McDougal, Littell

NONCONSUMABLE

Handwriting 2
Connections

ML McDougal, Littell & Company
Evanston, Illinois
New York • Dallas • Sacramento • Columbia, SC

Consultants

The following educators reviewed lessons during the development of the *Handwriting Connections* program.

Bettye S. Anderson, Teacher, Crestline Elementary School, Mountain Brook, Alabama

Lawrence Barretto, Teacher, Maplewood Elementary School, Coral Springs, Florida

Ruth Black, Curriculum Assistant for Writing; Chairperson, District 39 Language Arts Curriculum Review Committee; Wilmette Junior High School, Wilmette, Illinois

Mary K. Butcher, Teacher, Thomas Edison Elementary School, Port Huron, Michigan

Dr. Hazel S. Harvey, Elementary Curriculum Supervisor, Hillsborough County Schools, Tampa, Florida; Adjunct Professor, Nova University, Ft. Lauderdale, Florida

Sr. Paul Mary Janssens, O.P., Principal, St. Edward School, Chicago, Illinois

Nancy R. Lancaster, Language Arts Specialist, Escondido Union School District, Escondido, California

Phyllis M. Rantz, Principal, John E. Burke School, Peabody, Massachusetts

Christine Robertson, Principal, Bramble Elementary School, Cincinnati, Ohio

Ophelia Q. Smith, Teacher, J. J. Rhoads Elementary School, Houston, Texas

Debra Smith-Sokolowsky, Teacher, Kennedy Elementary School, Succasunna, New Jersey

Blossom Blackman Stobb, Grade-Level Chairman, Oak Meadow Elementary School, Northeast Indiana School District, San Antonio, Texas

Dahlia Tesher, Teacher, Jensen Scholastic Academy, Chicago, Illinois

Florence Viola, Teacher, St. Michael the Archangel School, Levittown, Pennsylvania

Multicultural Advisory Committee

Andrea B. Bermúdez, Professor of Multicultural Education; Director, Research Center for Language and Culture; University of Houston—Clear Lake

Martha Garland Livisay, Curriculum Specialist in Multi-ethnic Education, Ann Arbor, Michigan

Staff Credits

Sandra L. Corniels, Executive Editor
Marcia Crawford Mann, Senior Editor
Arnetta Carter, Editor
Robert C. St. Clair, Manager of Production
Susan V. Shorey, Production Coordinator
Ronald A. Rutkowski, Production Editor
Craig Jobson, Director of Design
Carol Tornatore, Senior Designer
Carmine Fantasia, Picture Editor

Special Contributors

Design Concepts
Design 5, New York, New York

Covers
Ryan Roessler, Cover Photography
Carol Tornatore, Cover Design

Acknowledgments

Isabel Joshlin Glaser: "Writing on the Chalkboard" by Isabel Joshlin Glaser, from *More Surprises,* Harper & Row, 1987. The author controls all rights.

ISBN 0–8123–7702–8
Copyright © 1993 McDougal, Littell & Company
Box 1667, Evanston, Illinois 60204
All rights reserved. Printed in the United States of America
1 2 3 4 5 6 7 8 9 10 – BMW – 96 95 94 93 92

Illustrations and Photography

Commissioned

Angela Adams: **11, 66, 67;** Elizabeth Allen: **8-9, 94, 95, 96, 97, 99 ;** Robert Alley: **28-29;** Lisa Berrett: **50, 62, 74, 79, 88;** Stephanie Britt: **35, 44, 51, 64, 79, 92, 105, 114;** Nan Brooks: **77, 84, 85, 89;** Rebecca D. Brown: *t* **1,** *t* **14,** *c* **15,** *t* **16, 20,** *c* **21,** *bc* **26,** *t* **27,** *t* **34, 45, 64, 65,** *c* **72, 93, 98, 112, 115;** Ralph J. Brunke: **3, 4, 5, 10, 22, 23,** *ur* **33, 47, 53, 92, 93, 96, 100, 111, 118, 122, 123, 126, 127, 139;** Maryann Cocca: *l, r* **34, 52, 53;** Brian Cody: **12;** Barbara Garrison: *b* **40, 82;** Doreen Gay-Kassel: **112;** Linda Graves: **43, 113;** Paul Harvey: **122;** Jean Helmer-Cassels: **22, 23, 24, 25,** *cl, cr* **41, 46, 47, 48, 49, 54, 55;** Steve Henry: **86, 87, 100, 101, 102, 103, 104;** Pat Hoggan: **91, 123;** Brian Karas: **106, 107, 111;** Elliot Kreloff: *c* **30,** *c* **31;** Benton Mahan: *ul, ur, b* **15;** Diane McKnight: **56, 57;** Carol Nicklaus: *c* **16, 18-19;** Linda Reilly: **70, 71;** Bruce Sereta: **6, 7, 10, 66, 67, 77;** Jerry Smath: *r* **72, 73;** Keith Spears: **42;** Susan Swan: *all ul* **28, 29, 30, 31, 32, 33, 36, 37, 38, 39, 40, 41, 46, 47, 48, 49, 52, 53, 54, 55, 58, 59, 60, 61, 66, 67, 68, 69, 74, 75, 76, 77, 80, 81, 82, 83, 86, 87, 88, 89, 94, 95, 98, 99, 100, 101, 104, 105, 106, 107, 110, 111, 112, 113, 118, 119, 120, 121, 122, 123, 124, 125, 126, 127, 132, 133, 134, 135, 136, 137, 138, 139, 142, 143, 144, 145, 146, 147, 148, 149;** Peggy Tagel: *b* **36, 116, 117;** Mary Thelen: *t* **38, 39, 56, 57;** Robert Voights: **1,** *b* **14,** *c* **34, 112, 117;** Rhonda Voo: **75, 78;** Linda Weller: *r* **21;** David Wenzel: **2, 3, 63;** Carl Whiting: **76, 80.**

Stock Photography

1: © Jeffrey Cadge/The Image Bank; **17:** Steve Bourgeois; **20:** *ur* © John Gerlach/Tom Stack & Associates; **21:** *ur* © John Gerlach/Tom Stack & Associates; **22:** *lr* © Manuel Rodriguez/The Image Bank; **26:** *ll* © Tony Freeman/PhotoEdit; **27:** *ur* © Tony Freeman/Photo Edit; **37:** © Werner Bokelberg/The Image Bank; **50:** Thomas Hovland/Grant Heilman Photography; **51:** © Ron Kimball; **63:** ©1987 Chris Springmann/The Stock Market; **79:** © LaFOTO/H. Armstrong Roberts; **81:** © Moos/Hake-Greenberg/Peter Arnold, Inc.; **88:** © Frank Oberle/Photo Researchers, Inc.; **104, 105, 106, 107:** NASA; **112:** C. Bryant/H. Armstrong Roberts; **113:** ©1990 Mark E. Gibson; **117:** © Elyse Lewin/The Image Bank; **132:** © Nik Wheeler/West Light.

Contents

UNIT 4 Getting Ready to Write Cursive 63

UNIT 5 Writing to Learn *Handwriting Focus: Spacing and Slant* 79

UNIT 6 Writing to Celebrate *Handwriting Focus: Smoothness* 117

SCHOOL BUS

EMERGENCY EXIT

Top Line	
Midline	*manuscript*
Baseline	
Descender Line	

Read the poem "Writing on the Chalkboard" by Isabel Joshlin Glaser.

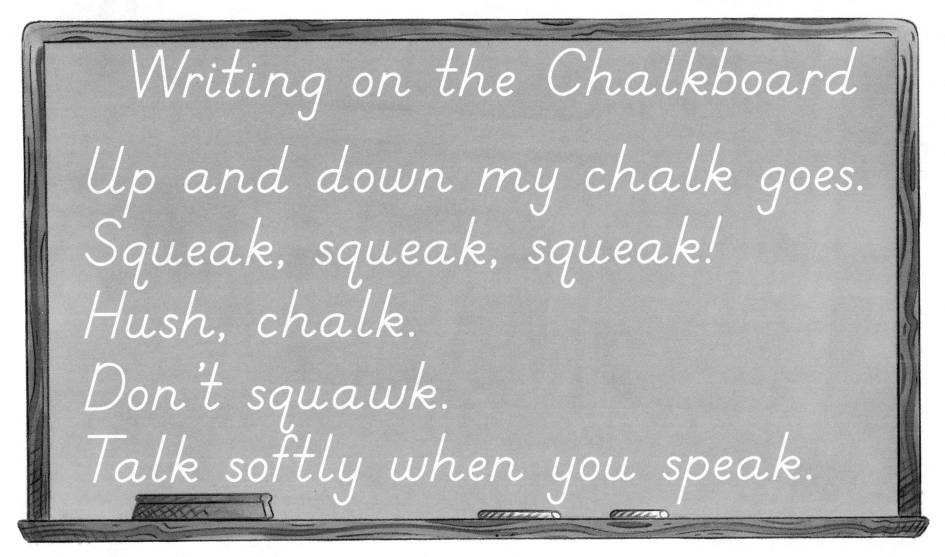

Writing on the Chalkboard

Up and down my chalk goes.
Squeak, squeak, squeak!
Hush, chalk.
Don't squawk.
Talk softly when you speak.

Copy the poem on page 2, beginning with the title. Use your best handwriting.

Write on your own paper.

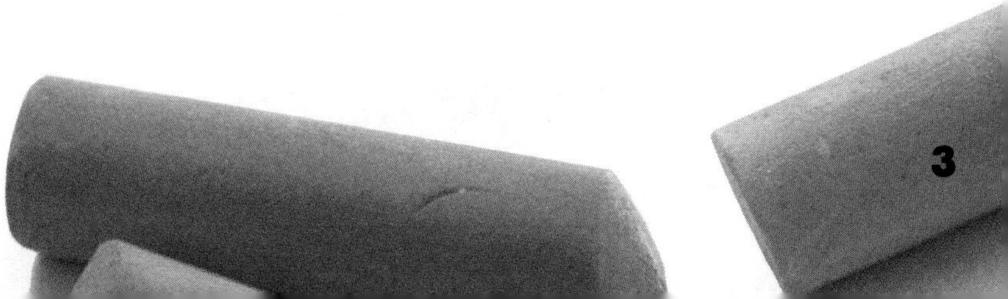

3

Letters can be made to look different.
Here is how the letters might look in the books you read.

Make a finger puppet.

This is how you would write the same sentence.

Make a finger puppet.

Tell how the letters are different.

4

The Manuscript Alphabet

A a   B b   C c   D d

E e   F f   G g   H h

I i   J j   K k   L l

M m   N n   O o   P p

Q q   R r   S s   T t

U u   V v   W w   X x

Y y   Z z

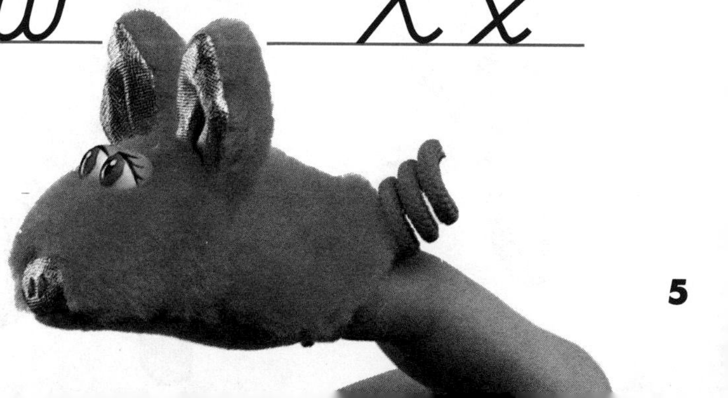

Sit tall.
Keep both feet on the floor.

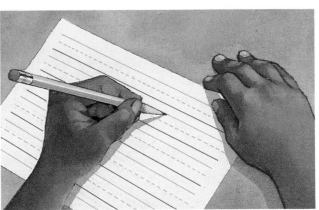

Slant your paper like this.
Hold your paper steady with your right hand.

Look at the picture. Then look at the way you hold your pencil. Do not hold your pencil too tightly.

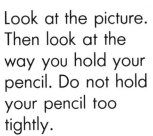

6

Right-handed Writers

Slant your paper like this.
Hold your paper steady
with your left hand.

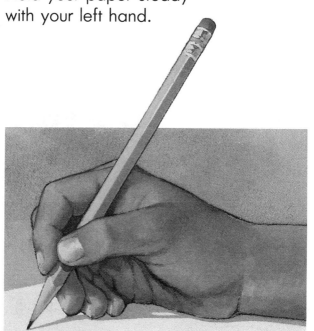

Look at the picture.
Then look at the
way you hold your
pencil. Do not hold
your pencil too
tightly.

Sit tall.
Keep both feet
on the floor.

7

Letter Shape

When letters are shaped correctly, words are easy to read.
Close up any ovals in letters like **a, g,** and **o.**

kangaroo   **NOT** kunyuroo

Cross **t**'s and **f**'s.

flutter   **NOT** fluller

Dot **i**'s and **j**'s.

juice   **NOT** juice

Tell what words are easy to read.   Do not write on this page.

terrific   juu   end

8

Letter Size

These are the names of the lines on which letters are written.

$G\,g$

Top line

Midline

Baseline

Descender line

These letters touch the top line.

$b \quad d \quad f \quad h \quad k \quad l \quad t$

These letters touch the midline.

$a \quad c \quad e \quad i \quad m \quad n \quad o \quad r \quad s \quad u \quad v \quad w \quad x \quad z$

These letters reach down below the baseline to the descender line.

$g \quad j \quad p \quad q \quad y$

Tell what word has letters three different sizes.

rain   tag   blocks

Letter and Word Spacing

Leave the space of a pencil point between letters.

octopus

Leave the space of a pencil between words.

a ship

Leave a finger space between sentences.

Come on! Swim with us.

Space letters evenly. Your writing will look better if you do.

Correct Spacing

my friend

Incorrect Spacing

mygo ldf i sh

Letter Slant and Smoothness

These are straight.

These are slanted.

rockets

globes

All your letters should slant in the same direction.

The spaceship landed.

Your letters should look smooth.
Smooth letters are easy to read.

Correct

Too dark

Too shaky

space

space

space

Write your numerals carefully.

0 1

1

2 2

3 3

4 4 4

Write on your own paper.

5 5 5

6

7 7

8

9 9

10   11   12

13   14   15

Copy each of these problems. Write every numeral in the right place.

Write on your own paper.

$7 + 8 = 15$ $2 + 4 = 6$

$+$ $=$ $+$ $=$

$3 + 6 = 9$ $7 + 5 = 12$

$+$ $=$ $+$ $=$

15 13
$+3$ $+$ $+4$ $+$
18 17

ON YOUR OWN   Write a math problem. Ask a partner to solve it.

A sentence that tells something is a **statement**. Use a period at the end of every statement.

Rafael collects rocks.

Write on your own paper.

I collect stickers.

Some words can be written in a shorter form called an **abbreviation**. Use a period after an abbreviation.

Monday Mon.

Street St.

14   **ON YOUR OWN**   Write a statement that tells something about you.

A sentence that asks something is a **question**.
Use a question mark at the end of a question.

? Write on your own paper. ? ?

Did you meet my puppy?

Can you count his spots?

Is Wags a good name?

 **SELF CHECK**   Circle the question mark you wrote at the end of each question.

15

Tell which letter has the correct shape.

b   q

Tell which letters reach down below the baseline.

y   t   p   e

Rewrite the sentence with the correct spacing.

Ise eyo u.

Write on your own paper.

Write the word so that the letters slant in the same direction.

pretend

Write this word smoothly.

aquarium

October 14

Dear Diary,

Today I caught a huge grasshopper!

Write on your own paper.

a _ _ _ _ _ _ _ *a* _ _ _ _ _ _ _ *a*

A _ _ _ _ _ _ _ A _ _ _ _ _ _ _ A

anthill   *crawling ants*

Ants are all around.

⭐ **SELF CHECK**   Circle your best A.

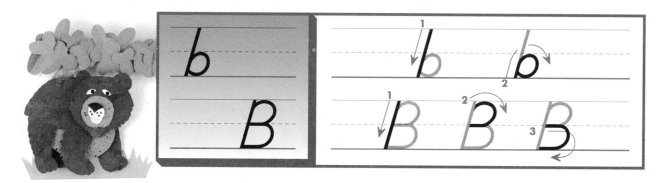

b

B

Write on your own paper.

b — — — — — *b* — — — — *b*

B — — — — — *B* — — — — *B*

best bug

Become a Bug Club member.

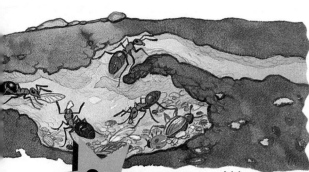

Be a buddy to a bug.

⭐ **ON YOUR OWN**   Write a sentence that describes your favorite bug.

19

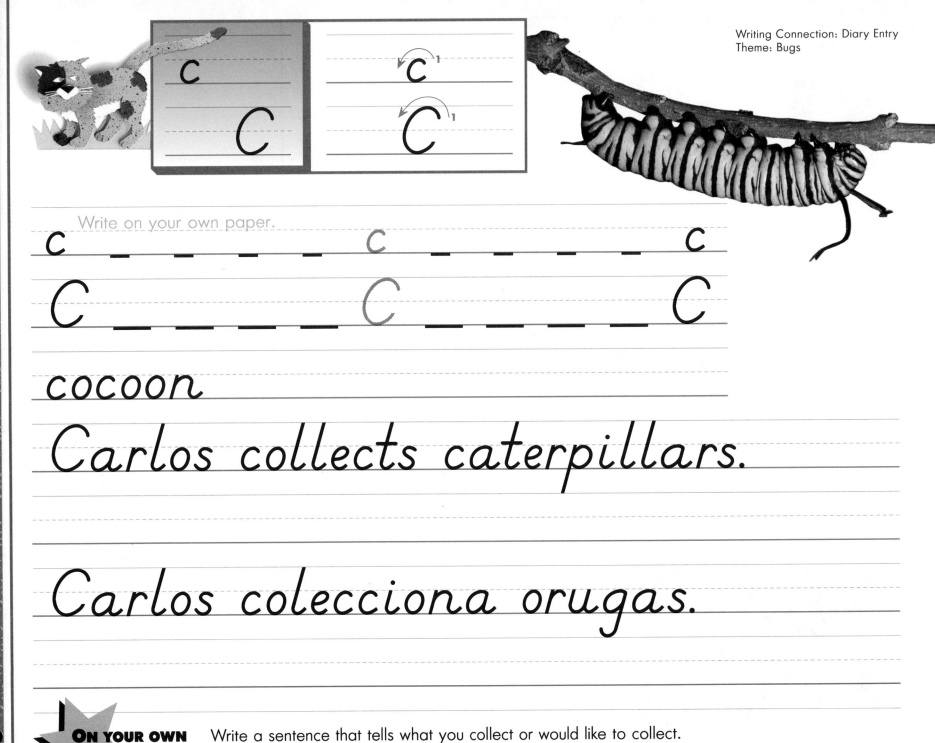

c   c   c

C   C   C

Write on your own paper.

cocoon

Carlos collects caterpillars.

Carlos colecciona orugas.

ON YOUR OWN Write a sentence that tells what you collect or would like to collect.

d *d* *d*

D *D* *D*

Write on your own paper.

d — — — *d* — — — *d*

D — — — *D* — — — *D*

different

Dragonflies are slender.

Daddy-longlegs are speedy.

★ **ASK A FRIEND** Have a friend circle your best *d*.

Linking Handwriting to Writing

Writing a Diary Entry

Read this entry from a Bug Club member's diary.

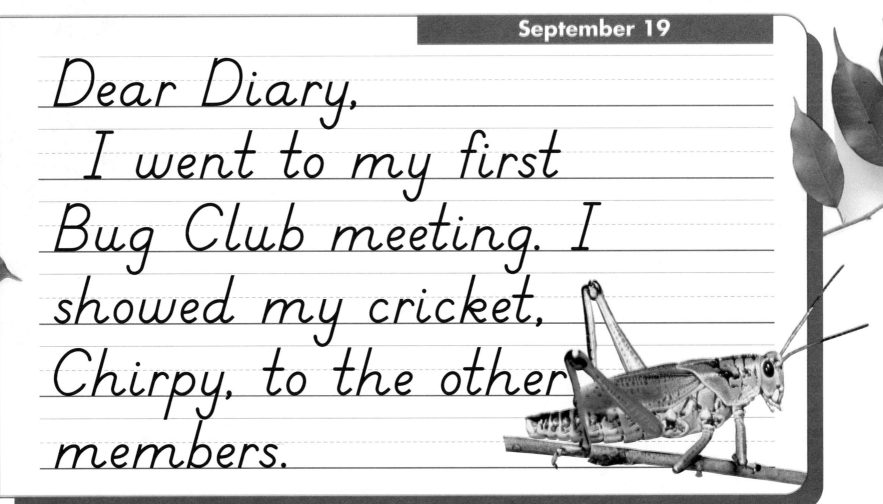

September 19

Dear Diary,
I went to my first
Bug Club meeting. I
showed my cricket,
Chirpy, to the other
members.

22   💻 **COMPUTER TIP**   When you complete a sentence, press the space bar two times after the punctuation.

Copy the diary entry.

September 19

Write on your own paper.

 **ON YOUR OWN**   How would Chirpy have described his day? Write a diary entry for him.

e

e

E

E E E

Write on your own paper.

e _ _ _ _ _ _ _ _ _ *e* _ _ _ _ _ _ _ _ *e*

E _ _ _ _ _ _ _ _ E _ _ _ _ _ _ _ _ E

everyone   here

Eva's family had a barbecue.

They enjoyed being together.

ON YOUR OWN   What do you and your relatives like to do together? Write about it.

24

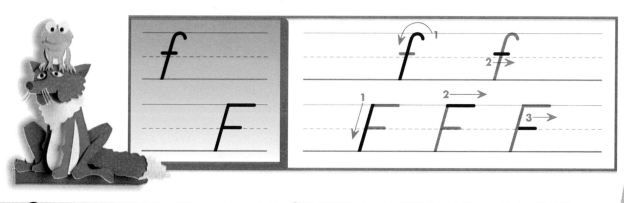

f   f

F   F

f   Write on your own paper.   *f*   *f*

F   *F*   *F*

Fernández family

Aunt Fran   Uncle Jeff

from Florida

ASK A FRIEND   Have a friend circle an *f* or *F* that you need to improve.

Writing Connection: Telephone List
Theme: Family Reunion

g
G

Write on your own paper.

g   g   g
G   G   G

Grown-ups gave lots of hugs.

Great-grandpa got hugs.

26   **SELF CHECK**   Circle a *g* that touches the descender line.

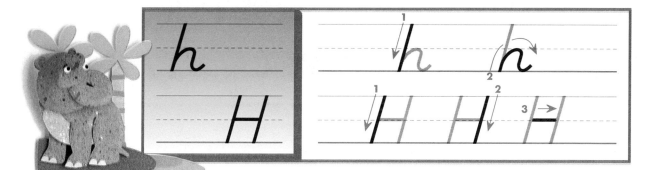

h   h   h

H   H   H

Write on your on paper.

home   reach

Hillary and Eva promised

to phone each other.

Writing a Telephone List

Copy what Eva wrote in a family telephone book she made.

F

Fernández

Fernández

Write on your own paper.

Hector
(713) 555-1912

Hillary
(419) 555-1621

Leah
(312) 555-4811

F

ON YOUR OWN   Make a list of the family members you call often. Put their names in alphabetical order.

Eva's cousin Sam helped out at the barbecue.
Copy his list of things to do.
Watch the sizes of your letters as you write.

1. Fill cups with milk.
2. Choose fruit for dessert.
3. Help do the dishes.

Write on your own paper.

Circle the letter you wrote best.

Circle a word in which all the letters are the correct size.

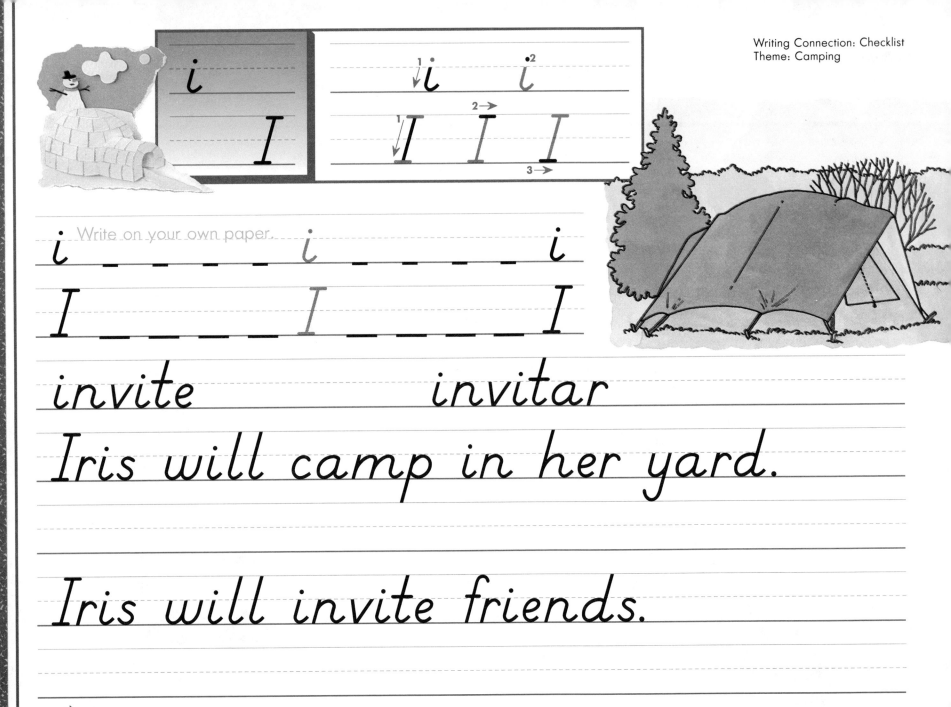

i

I

Write on your own paper.

i   i   i

I   I   I

invite   invitar

Iris will camp in her yard.

Iris will invite friends.

 SELF CHECK   Circle your best *i* 's.

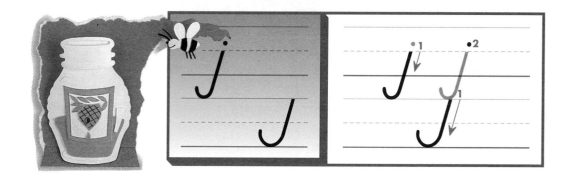

j   Write on your own paper.

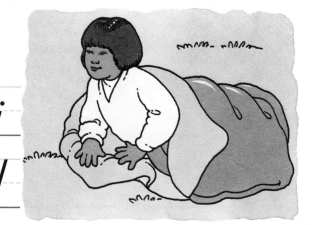

j   j   j

J   J   J

juice   el jugo

Jan's job is to make juice.

Jan enjoys camping.

ON YOUR OWN   Draw something you like to do. Write a sentence about your picture.

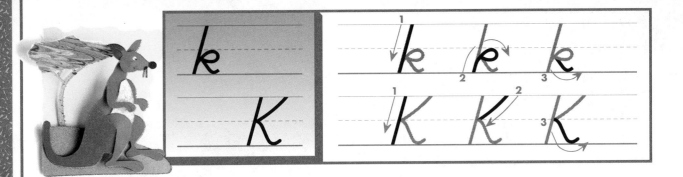

k

K

k _ _ _ _ _ _ k _ _ _ _ _ k

K _ _ _ _ _ _ K _ _ _ _ _ K

keep   guardar

Kim is taking her knapsack.

Kim likes to pack quickly.

  **ON YOUR OWN**   Write a sentence that tells what you think is in Kim's knapsack.

l

L

Write on your own paper.

l _ _ _ _ _ *l* _ _ _ _ *l*

L _ _ _ *L* _ _ _ *L*

list   la lista

Luis will make a checklist.

Luis will write carefully.

Checklist
1. tent
2. first-aid kit
3. trail mix
4. jackets

⭐ **ASK A FRIEND**   Have a friend circle your best *L* .

33

Writing a Checklist

Copy Luis's checklist of things for camping.

Checklist
1. tent
2. first-aid
kit
3. trail mix
4. jackets

Write on your own paper.

34   **ON YOUR OWN**   Imagine you could camp out on the moon. What would you take?

Anansi and the Tiger

What if Snake had escaped before Anansi could finish tying him to the bamboo? Write a new ending for the tale. Tell another way Anansi could catch Snake.

35

Iris has plans for a day at camp.
Copy this part of her schedule.
Watch the size of your letters as you write.

1:30   Hike to the lake.
2:30   Look for birds.
3:30   Decorate T-shirts.

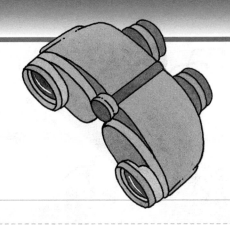

Circle the capital letter you wrote best.

Circle a word in which all the letters are the correct size.

My Blue Kite
My blue kite
soars high up
to the sky.

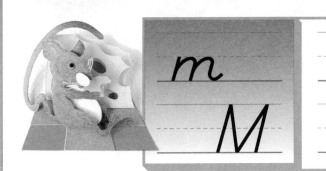

m
M

m m m
M M M M

Writing Connection: Story
Theme: Storybook Animals

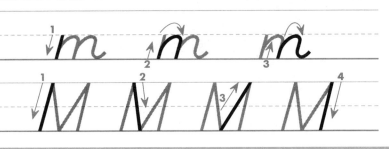

Write on your own paper.

m ____ ____ ____ ____ m ____ ____ ____ ____ m

M ____ ____ ____ ____ M ____ ____ ____ ____ M

Mimi monkey

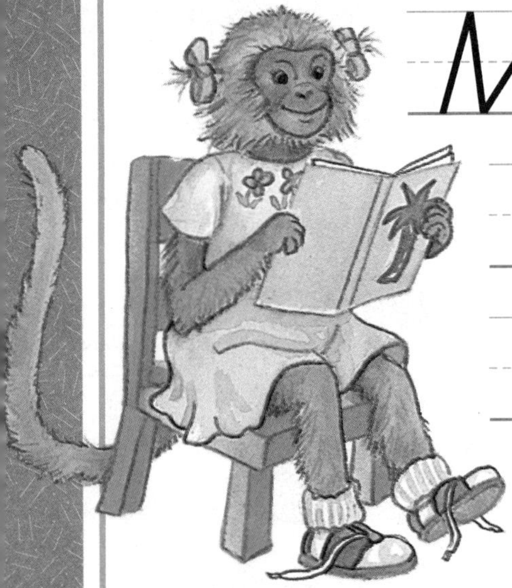

Make-believe animals may seem almost human.

SELF CHECK Circle your best m.

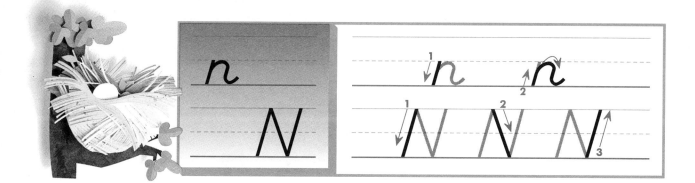

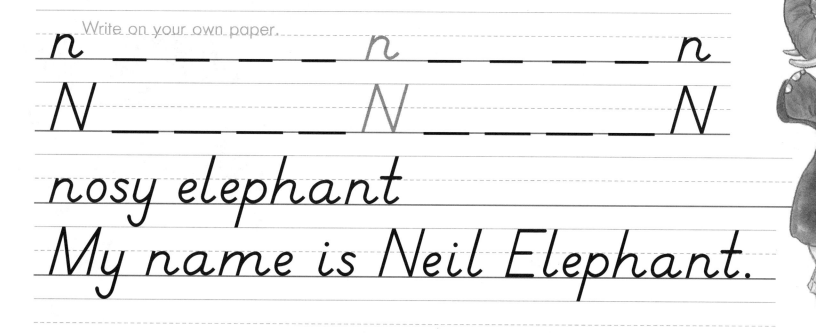

Write on your own paper.

n   *n*   *n*

N   *N*   *N*

nosy elephant

My name is Neil Elephant.

Mi nombre es Neil Elefante.

 **ON YOUR OWN**   Say the Spanish sentence, using your name.

39

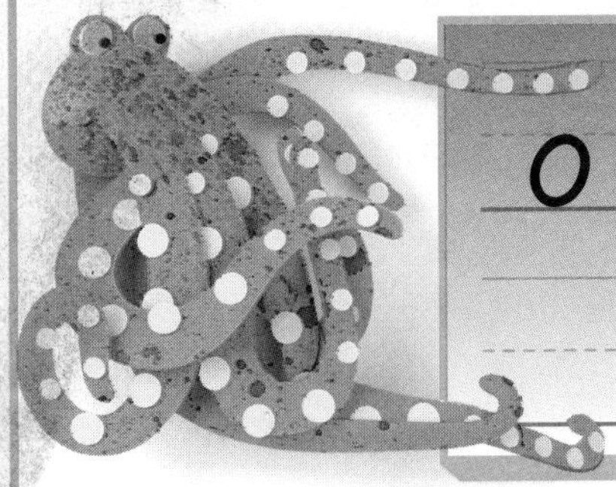

o   o   o   o

O   O   O   O   O

Write on your own paper.

o _ _ _ _ o _ _ _ _ o

O _ _ _ _ O _ _ _ _ O

Olga Owl
Owls in stories are
often old and wise.

40

 **ASK A FRIEND**   Have a friend circle an O that is closed.

P

Write on your own paper.

P

P

porcupine

Percy is unhappy.

Perhaps Olga can help.

ON YOUR OWN   Write a sentence that a storybook animal might say.

Linking Handwriting to Writing

Writing a Story

Proofreading Read the story below. Tell what proofreading marks are needed to correct capital letters and periods.

Proofreading Marks

≡ Use a capital letter. ted.

⊙ Add a period. Go now⊙

Tell where the mistakes are.

Percy Porcupine was sad. no one could hug him. He had sharp quills One day his friends came to help. olga Owl had an idea

42

Final Draft Copy the story. Make the corrections that your proofreading marks show.

HANDWRITING TIP Remember to close all your *o*'s and O's.

Write on your own paper.

ON YOUR OWN Finish the story. Tell what you think Olga Owl's idea is.

43

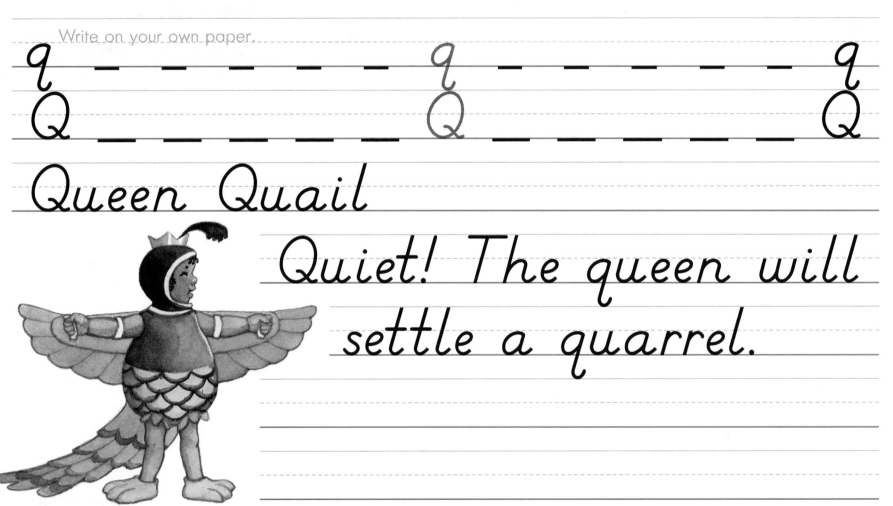

Write on your own paper.

q
Q

q
Q

q
Q

Queen Quail

Quiet! The queen will settle a quarrel.

44 ⭐ **ASK A FRIEND**   Have a friend circle any *q* that needs to be made better because it looks like a *g*.

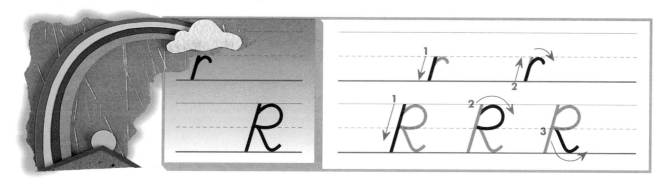

r   r

R   R

Write on your own paper.

r _ _ _ _ r _ _ _ r

R _ _ _ _ R _ _ _ R

read parts

Roberto will play a rude

rabbit named Rufus.

 **ON YOUR OWN**   Write a sentence telling what problem a rude rabbit might have.

45

s S

Write on your own paper.

s   s   s

S   S   S

a snake

Sara plays a smart snake.

She hisses as she speaks.

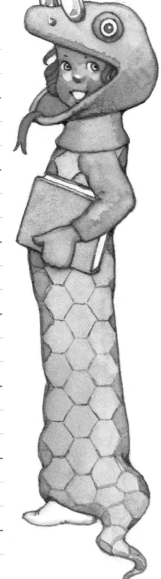

  **ON YOUR OWN**   Make a list of other words that describe a snake.

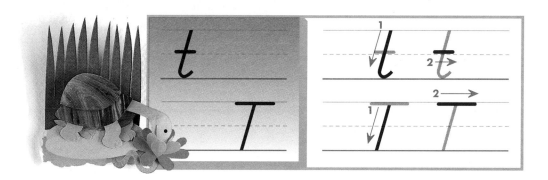

t *t* *t*

T *T* *T*

Write on your own paper.

timid tiger

Tell Titus to talk

very softly.

 **SELF CHECK** Circle a *t* that touches the top line and is crossed.

47

Linking Handwriting to Writing

Writing a Play

Copy these lines from a story that is written as a play.
Be sure to write the names of the characters.

Queen.   What's wrong?

Write on your own paper.

Snake.   Rufus hides things!

Tiger.   Tell him to quit.

48   **ON YOUR OWN**   Write a sentence telling what Rufus might say. Then write a sentence telling how the problem with Rufus might be solved.

Copy the beginning of the story
"The Shoemaker and the Elves."
Try to shape each letter correctly.

Quite a long time ago, a
shoemaker had leather for
only one pair of shoes.

Write on your own paper.

Circle the letter
you wrote best.

Circle a word you
wrote that has all the
letters shaped correctly.

49

Write on your own paper.

u   u   u

U   U   U

munch   quack

Animal sounds are fun.

Use them in your poems.

50   ★ **ON YOUR OWN**   Make a list of animals and the sounds each one makes.

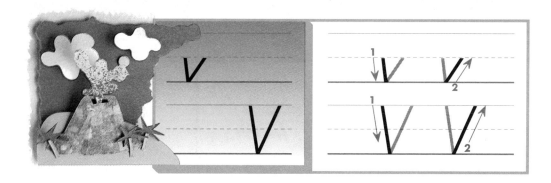

v v v

V V V

Write on your own paper.

v   v   v

V   V   V

Velvet

Lively eyes,
Silver fur,
Very soft,
I love her.

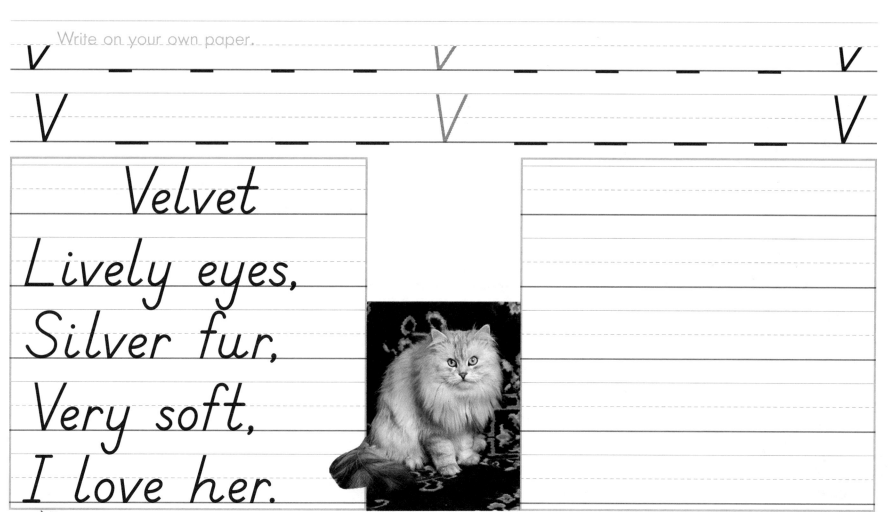

 **SELF CHECK** Circle your best *v* and *V*.

51

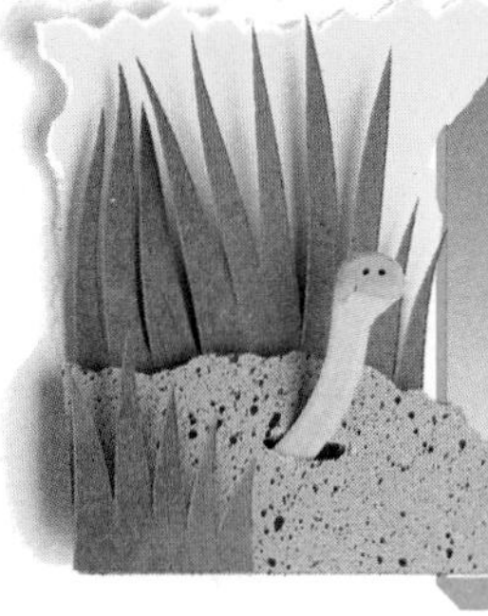

w W

Writing Connection: Poem
Theme: Animals

w w

W W W W

Write on your own paper.

w _ _ _ _ w _ _ _ _ w

W _ _ _ W _ _ _ W

Write words that rhyme.

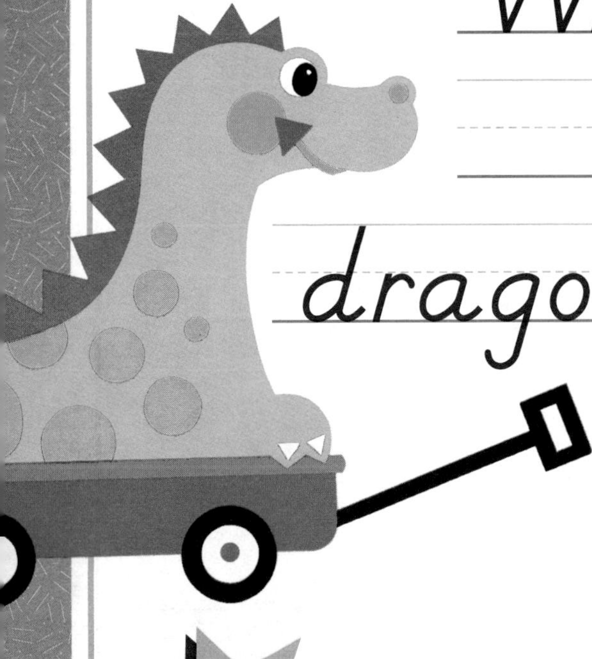

dragon wagon

slow crow

pale whale

ON YOUR OWN Make a list of words that rhyme with *way*.

x

X

Write on your own paper.

x _____ *x* _____ *x*

X _____ *X* _____ *X*

Xavier's poem

Max, a boy,
has a toy.
It's a fox
in a box!

⭐ **ASK A FRIEND**   Ask a classmate to circle your best *x*.

53

Writing a Poem

Copy the title, the author's name, and the four lines of "The Little Turtle"
on the next page. As you write, use words in place of the pictures.
Look at the Word Box to find the words you need.

The Little Turtle

by Vachel Lindsay

There was a little

He lived in a

He swam in a

He climbed on the

WORD BOX

box   puddle   rocks   turtle

Write on your own paper.

 **ON YOUR OWN**   Think of other words that rhyme with *box*. Write a new last line for the poem.

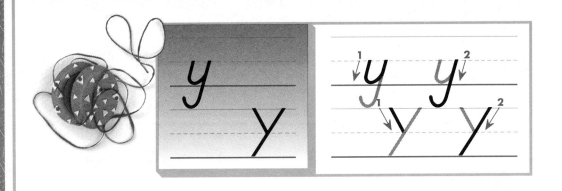

y
Y

Write on your own paper.

y — — — — — y — — — — — y
Y — — — — — Y — — — — — Y

yummy honey

Furry Bear loves honey.

You may like honey, too.

  SELF CHECK   Circle your best y and Y.

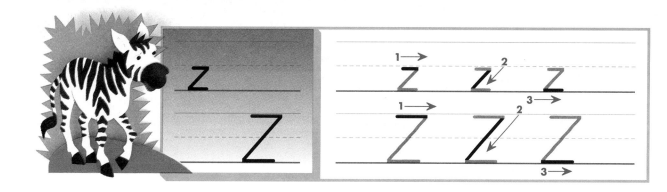

Write on your own paper.

z _ _ _ _ _ _ _ _ z _ _ _ _ _ _ _ _ z

Z _ _ _ _ _ _ _ Z _ _ _ _ _ _ _ _ Z

zooms   buzzes

Zippy Bee zooms and buzzes.

Zippy likes to save his honey.

ON YOUR OWN   Make a list of silly words that begin with **Z** or have **Z** in them.

57

Linking Handwriting to Writing

Writing a Cartoon

Look at the cartoon below and at the three words in the box.
Write the word that should go in each cartoon balloon.

Yeow!   Yum!   Buzz.

Write on your own paper.

58 ⭐ **ON YOUR OWN**   Draw pictures to show what happens next. Write words to tell what the bear and the bee say.

Handwriting Problems

Sometimes handwriting is not easy to read. You can improve your handwriting by learning the reasons for handwriting problems.

Causes of Handwriting Problems

1. not closing letters   *jacket*   *jacket*

2. closing looped letters   *idgi*   *edge*

3. creating loops in letters with no loops   *qeeickly*   *quickly*

4. using straight strokes instead of round ones   *cauper*   *camper*

Write this sentence in your best handwriting. Keep the handwriting problems in mind as you check your work.

Look at the bear.

Write on your own paper.

The Three Billy Goats Gruff

Pretend you are a reporter who interviews the Three Billy Goats Gruff after they have crossed the bridge. Write a question for one of the billy goats. Then write the goat's answer.

Copy the English version or the Spanish version
of this poem, "Beautiful Butterfly."
Try to shape each letter correctly.

English
Shining butterfly,
Butterfly of pure gold,
On its wings a treasure,
Flying butterfly.

Spanish
Mariposa luminosa,
Mariposa de puro oro,
En las alas un tesoro,
Mariposa voladora.

Write on your own paper.

Circle your best letter.

Circle a word you wrote that has all the letters shaped correctly.

Copy the poem ''Writing on the Chalkboard'' by Isabel Joshlin Glaser on your own paper.
Begin with the title. Use your best handwriting.

Writing on the Chalkboard
Up and down, my chalk goes.
Squeak, squeak, squeak!
Hush, chalk.
Don't squawk.
Talk softly when you speak.

Cursive is fun!

Cursive is fun!

Two Alphabets

How are the letters in each pair alike? How are they different?

a a   b b   c c   d d

e e   f f   g g   h h

i i   j j   k k   l l

m m   n n   o o   p p

q q   r r   s s   t t

u u   v v   w w   x x

y y   z z

Two Alphabets

AA BB CC DD
EE FF GG HH
II JJ KK LL
MM NN OO PP
QQ RR SS TT
UU VV WW XX
YY ZZ

Sit tall.
Keep both feet on the floor.

Slant your paper like this. Hold your paper steady with your right hand.

Look at the picture. Then look at the way you hold your pencil. Do not hold your pencil too tightly.

Right-handed Writers

Slant your paper like this.
Hold your paper steady
with your left hand.

Sit tall.
Keep both feet
on the floor.

Look at the picture.
Then look at the
way you hold your
pencil. Do not hold
your pencil too
tightly.

67

Matching Manuscript and Cursive Letters

Draw lines to match cursive and manuscript letters.

Write on your own paper.

m	v	p	q	l	l
v	n	q	g	b	h
u	u	g	p	h	b
D	O	H	R	Y	J
O	S	R	K	?	Z
S	D	K	H	J	Y

Teacher Note: This page may be reproduced for classroom use.

Matching Manuscript and Cursive Words

Read the word in the box. Circle the word that matches it.

Write on your own paper.

bear	hear	bear	dear
went	went	west	want
fan	far	pan	fan
skate	shake	skate	slate
meat	meat	meal	neat

Recognizing Cursive Letters

Read each cursive letter. Print the manuscript letter that matches it.   Write on your own paper.

a	a	*t*		*j*	
o		*k*		*g*	
s		*b*		*x*	
C		*T*		*W*	
I		*L*		*M*	
E		*F*		*Q*	

Recognizing Cursive Words

Read each cursive word. Print it in manuscript. Write on your own paper.

say   _say_

Carl   _____

mop   _____

buzz   _____

have   _____

quit   _____

king   _____

fox   _____

jaw   _____

Dee   _____

71

Comparing Manuscript and Cursive Letters

Many manuscript and cursive letters look very much alike. Look at
the letters below. Tell how each manuscript letter was changed
to make a cursive letter.

Manuscript   h   k   l   t   a   d   m   n

Cursive   h   k   l   t   a   d   m   n

These manuscript and cursive letters do not look very much alike.
Can you name the letters in the cursive row?

Manuscript   b   f   r   s   v   z

Cursive   b   f   r   s   v   z

Undercurve Connections

Many cursive letters begin with a stroke called an undercurve. An undercurve looks a little like an ocean wave.

Try making some undercurves. Notice that they can be short or tall.

Write on your own paper.

When you add an undercurve to these manuscript letters, you make cursive letters.

e h i j k l p t u w y

Look at how undercurve letters connect.

h i l l   hill   k i t e   kite

Overcurve Connections

Some cursive letters begin with a stroke called an overcurve.
An overcurve looks a little like part of a hill.

Practice making overcurves.

Write on your own paper.

When you add an overcurve to the beginning of these
manuscript letters, you make cursive letters.

a c d g m n o q v x

Look at how these overcurve letters connect.

c a n can   a d d add

Cross-Stroke Connections

Some letters **end** with a special stroke called a cross stroke. A cross stroke looks a little like a bridge.

Practice making cross strokes.

Write on your own paper.

These letters end with a cross stroke.

b o v w

When a cross stroke is used to connect two letters, the shape of the second letter changes. Look at how the letters change.

o n on one

w e we wet

Cursive writing slants.

Cursive writing slants.

All your letters should slant in the same direction.

The letters slant correctly.

Do not slant letters in different directions.
Your writing may not be easy to read.

What is wrong here?

Spacing in Cursive Writing

Leave the space of a pencil point between letters.

mouse

Leave the space of a pencil between words.

my dog

Leave a finger space between sentences.

What is that? It is a cat.

Space letters and words evenly. Your writing will look better if you do.

Correct spacing

his frog

Incorrect spacing

her fish

Read each cursive word. Print it in manuscript.

how   Write on your own paper.   sit

Ann   Mel

Tell which words slant correctly.

mice   hill   went

late   said   bend

Tell which words have letters that are spaced correctly.

about   many   read   little

Writing to Learn

Book Report
<u>Circus Life</u> by Ima Clown
is about circus clowns. It
tells how clowns get ready
for circuses.

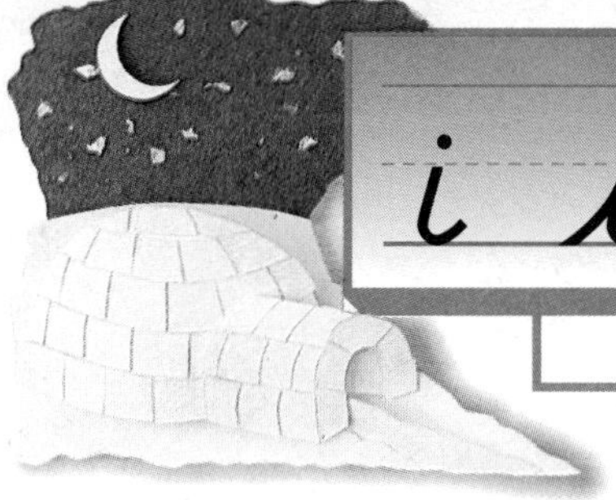

i i

1 *i* 2 *i* 3 *i*

Writing Connection: Word Web
Theme: Circus

i

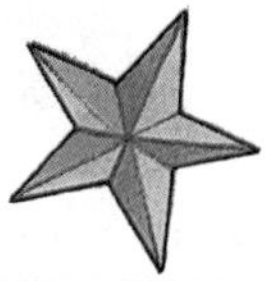

Write on your own paper.

i _ _ _ _ _ *i* _ _ _ _ _ *i*

i _ _ _ _ _ *i* _ _ _ _ _ *i*

i _ _ _ _ _ *i* _ _ _ _ _ *i*

ii i i ii

ii

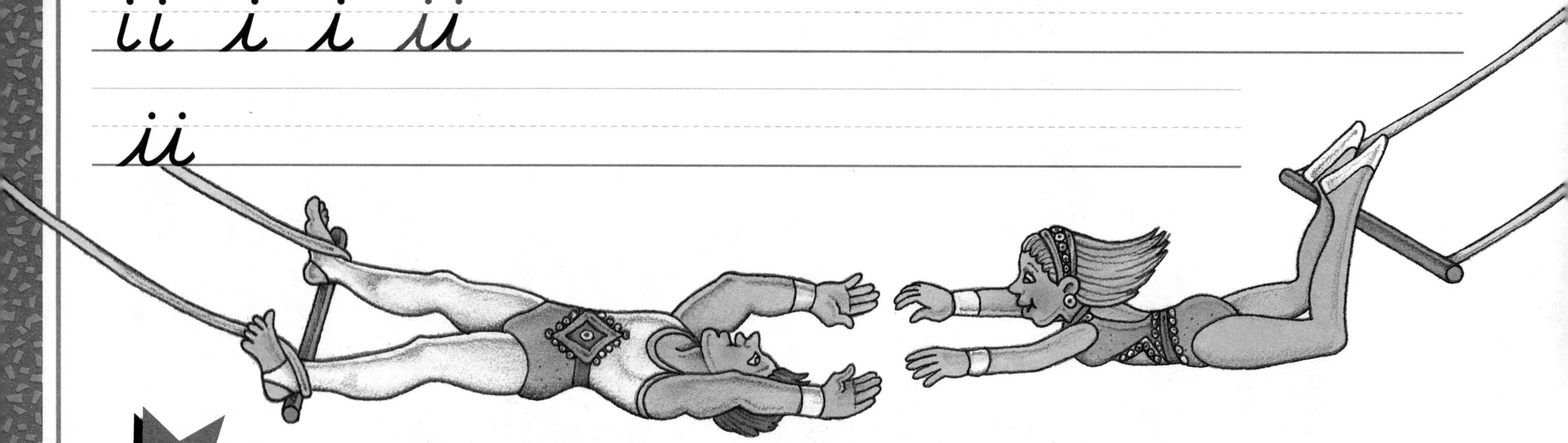

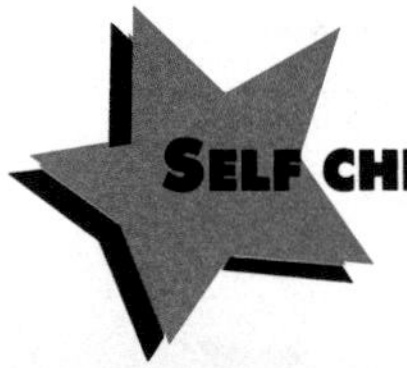

SELF CHECK Circle your best *i*.

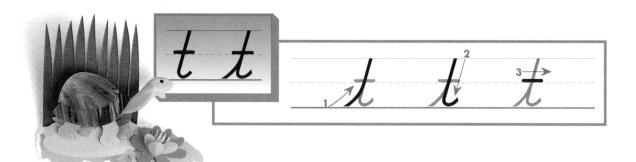

t t

1 t 2 t 3 t

t

t Write on your own paper. t t

t t t

t t t

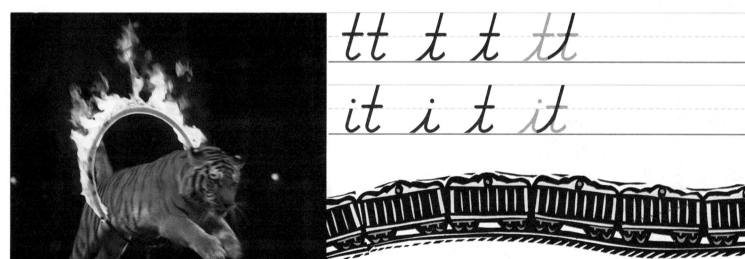

tt t t tt

it i t it

⭐ **ON YOUR OWN** Draw a picture of your favorite circus animal.

81

u *u*

u

Write on your own paper.

u _ _ _ _ _ _ *u* _ _ _ _ _ *u*

u _ _ _ _ _ _ *u* _ _ _ _ _ *u*

ut *u* *t* *ut*

tu *t* *u* *tu*

tutu *tutu*

82 ★ ON YOUR OWN   Write two words that tell about clowns.

_s s_

_s   s   s_

_s_

Write on your own paper.

_s _ _ _ _ _ s _ _ _ _ _ s_

_s _ _ _ _ _ s _ _ _ _ _ s_

ss s s ss

si s i si

su s u su

sit sit

suit suit

⭐ **ASK A FRIEND**   Have a friend circle an _s_ that slants correctly.

83

e *e*

e

e

Write on your own paper.

e _ _ _ _ _ _ _ *e* _ _ _ _ _ _ _ *e*

e _ _ _ _ _ _ _ *e* _ _ _ _ _ _ _ *e*

ee *e* *e* *ee*

se *s* *e* *se*

see *see*

set *set*

use *use*

ASK A FRIEND   Have a friend circle any *e* that looks like an uncrossed *t*.

ℓ ℓ ℓ

ℓ ℓ

ℓ Write on your own paper. ℓ ℓ

ℓ ℓ ℓ

$\ell\ell$ ℓ ℓ $\ell\ell$

ℓi ℓ i ℓi

little little

tilt tilt

stilts stilts

ON YOUR OWN   What's the most amazing thing you might see at a circus? Draw an amazing circus scene.

85

r r

r

Write on your own paper.

r   r   r

r   r   r

ri ri rise rise

tr tr tries tries

rise

tries

true

SELF CHECK   Circle the word you wrote best.

86

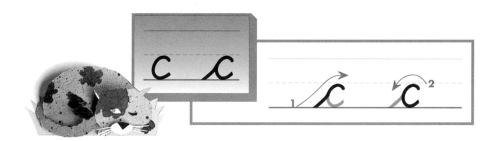

c C

c

Write on your own paper.

c _____ c _____ c

c _____ c _____ c

ci *ci*   circus *circus*

cl *cl*   circle *circle*

_____ circus circle_

⭐ **ON YOUR OWN**   Make up a riddle about a circus animal. Have a friend answer your riddle.

87

a a

$\mathcal{a}$ $\mathcal{a}^2$ $\mathcal{a}^3$

a

Write on your own paper.

a _____ a _____ a

a _____ a _____ a

al al   all all

ar ar   star star

ea ea   seal seal

a seal act

 **ASK A FRIEND**   Have a friend circle your best a.

d d d d

Write on your own paper.

d _____ d _____ d

d _____ d _____ d

di di   did did

de de   ride ride

ad ad   add add

rider rides

ON YOUR OWN   The horses whinny. The elephants trumpet.
Make a circus sound or describe one to a partner.

89

Linking Handwriting to Writing

Writing a Word Web

Copy the circus word web.

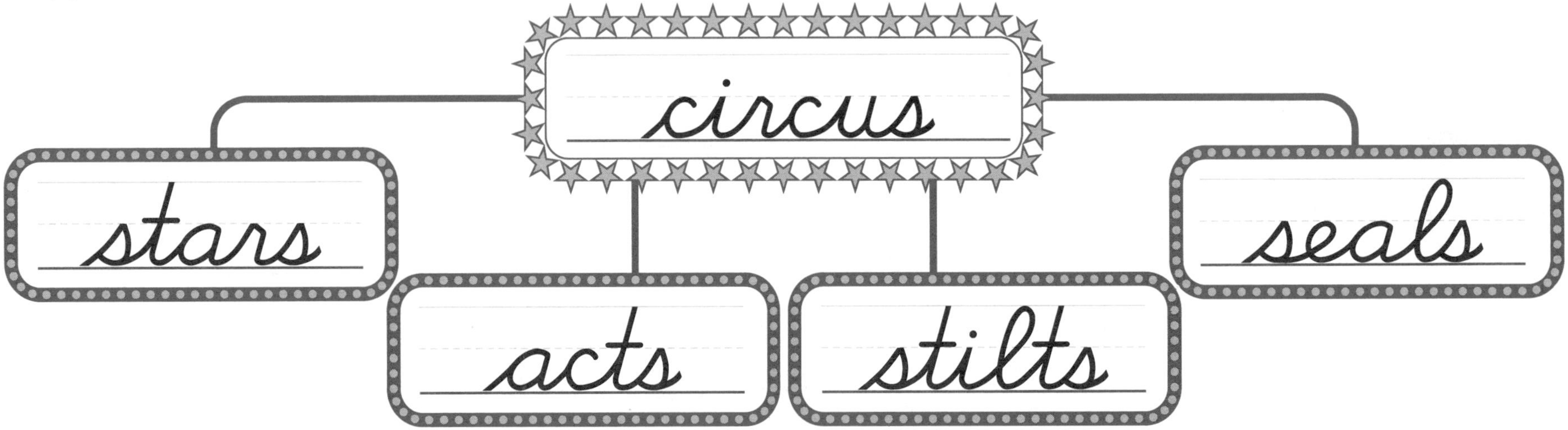

circus

stars

acts

stilts

seals

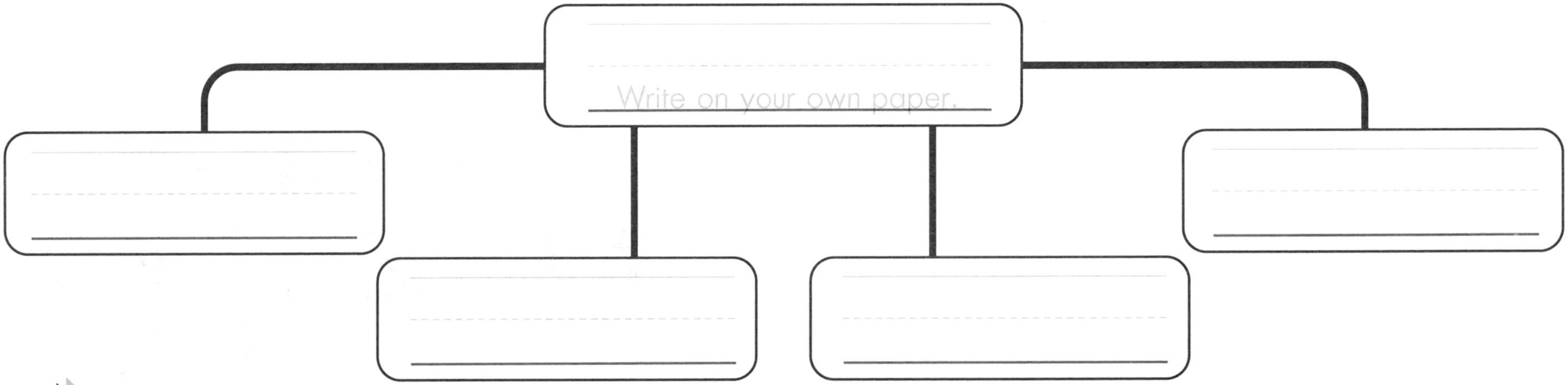

Write on your own paper.

  **ON YOUR OWN** Think of more circus words to add to the word web.

Copy these phrases. Remember to use your best cursive handwriting.

true circus stars

real creatures

still a success

Write on your own paper.

Circle a word you spaced correctly.

Circle a word in which all the letters slant correctly.

91

o o o

o

Write on your own paper.

o _ _ _ _ _ _ o _ _ _ _ _ o

o _ _ _ _ _ _ o _ _ _ _ _ o

oo o o oo   toot

recorder

caramillo

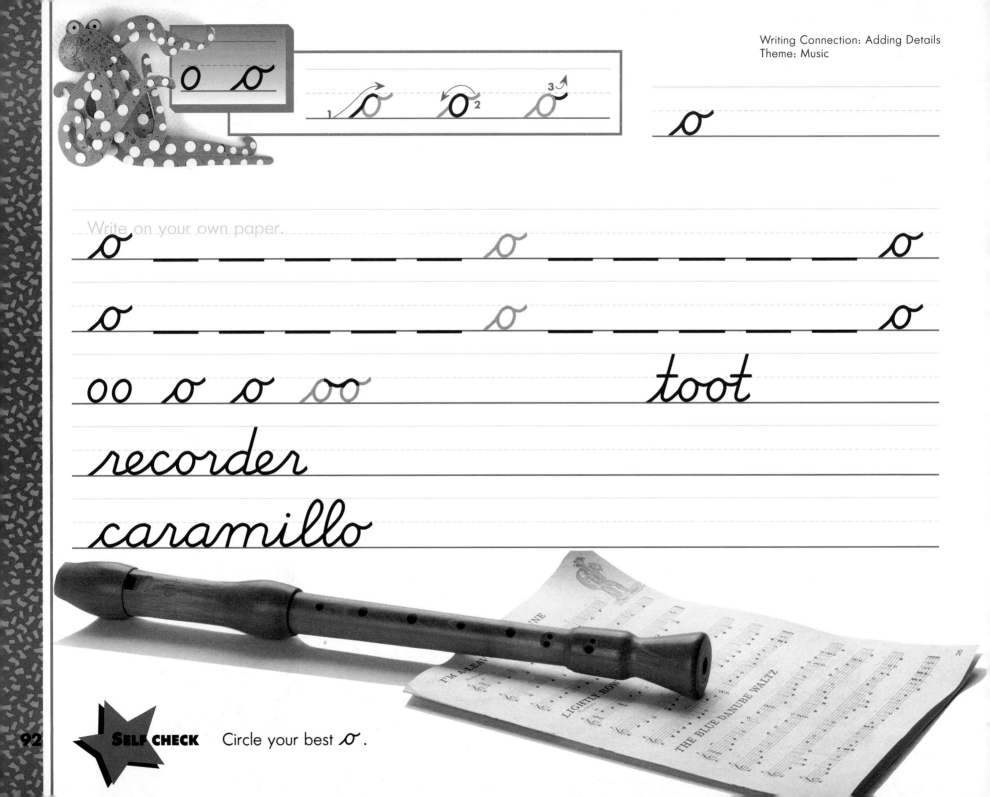

SELF CHECK   Circle your best *o*.

g g

g

g

Write on your own paper.

g — — — g — — — g

g — — — g — — — g

guitar guitar

la guitarra

guitar guide

ON YOUR OWN

How do you feel when you're listening to your favorite music?
Share your feelings with a partner.

93

m m

m m m

m

Write on your own paper.

m _____ m _____ m

m _____ m _____ m

music music

om o m om

some more music

ON YOUR OWN Roll modeling clay into long, thin strips. Use the strips of clay to form the cursive letter m.

n m

n n

n

Write on your own paper.

n _____ n _____ n

n _____ n _____ n

notes notes

un u n un   tune

notes in a song

⭐ **ASK A FRIEND**   Have a friend circle any *n*'s that do not have rounded tops.

Linking Handwriting to Writing

Writing to Add Details

Proofreading The box shows proofreading marks you can use to correct mistakes or to add more details.

Notice how proofreading marks are used with these details about a song.

Proofreading Marks	
∧	Add words.
—	Take out words.

a ~a~ song

comical
a ∧ song

long,
a ∧ comical song

loud
a ∧ long, comical song

96 💻 **COMPUTER TIP**   Look closely at a computer keyboard. Find the key that helps you delete, or take out letters or words. Find the key that helps you insert, or put in, letters or words.

Final Draft   Copy the details about a song from the previous page. Make the corrections that the proofreading marks show.

HANDWRITING TIP   Remember to connect the letters of the words.

Write on your own paper.

ON YOUR OWN   If you wrote a loud, long, comical song, what would it be about? Write a title for your song and share it with a classmate.

97

h

Write on your own paper.

h _ _ _ _ _ _ *h* _ _ _ _ _ _ *h*

h _ _ _ _ _ _ *h* _ _ _ _ _ _ *h*

hear hear

hoot hoot

hearing hoots

SELF CHECK Circle a word you spaced correctly.

k k

1 k 2 k 3 k

k

k _____ k _____ k

k _____ k _____ k

knock knock

tick tick

ticktock clock

ON YOUR OWN   List things that make knocking or ticking sounds.

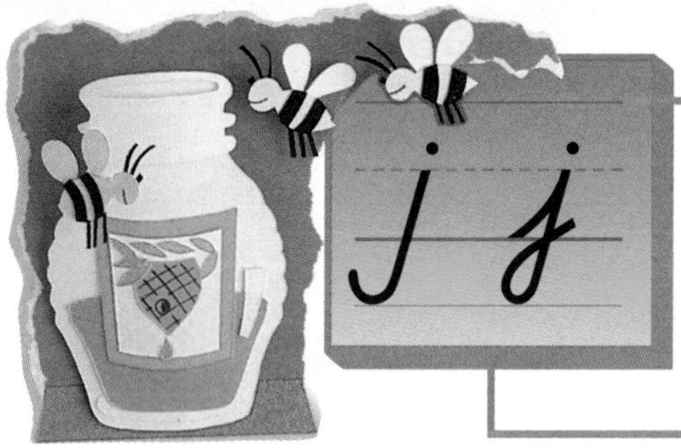

Writing Connection: Learning Log
Theme: Sounds

j j

j j j

j

Write on your own paper.

j j j

j j j

jingle jingle

jiggle to jingle

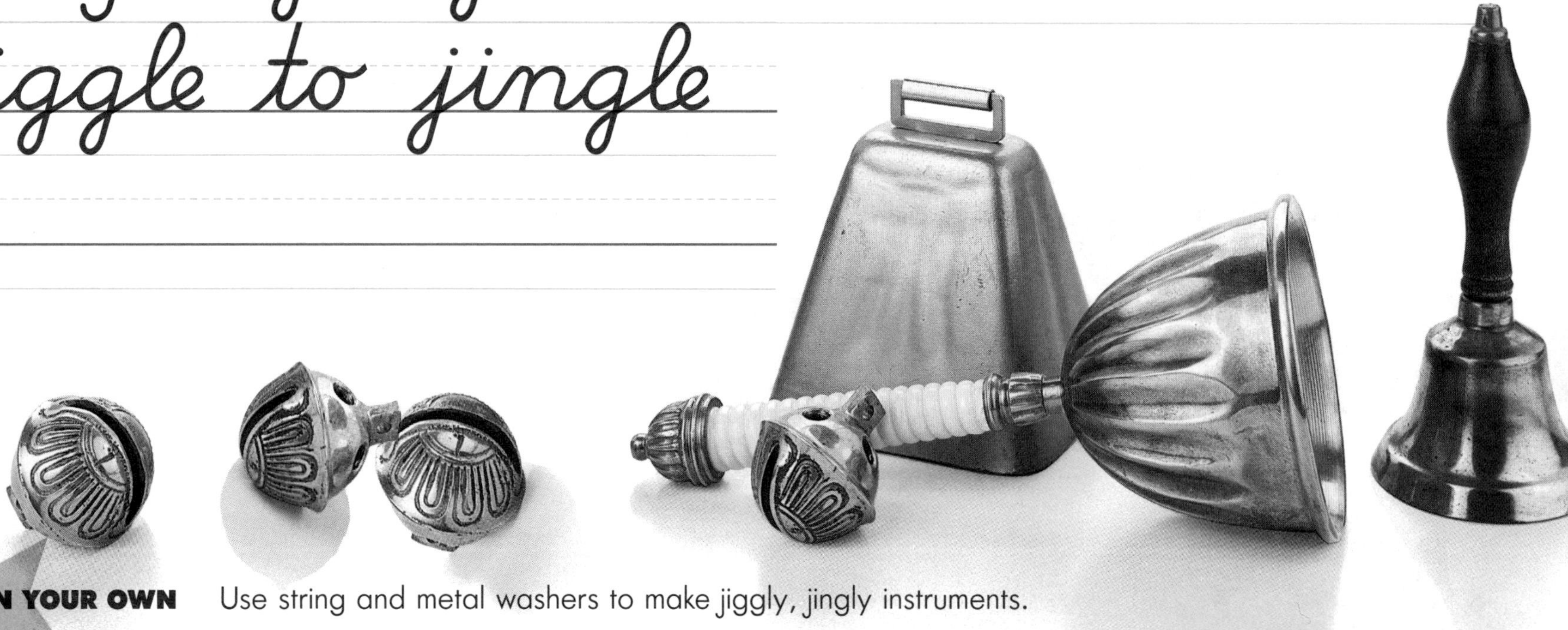

ON YOUR OWN Use string and metal washers to make jiggly, jingly instruments.

y y

y y²

y

Write on your own paper.

y _ _ _ _ _ _ y _ _ _ _ _ y

y _ _ _ _ _ _ y _ _ _ _ _ y

yell yell

noisy noisy

youngsters yelling

ASK A FRIEND   Have a friend circle your best y.

Linking Handwriting to Writing

Writing a Learning Log

Copy the information in the learning log below.

animal sounds

cluck, roar, moo, hiss,

rustle, coo, oink

Write on your own paper.

102

ON YOUR OWN Think about your favorite sound. Discuss with an adult what causes that sound.

Copy these phrases. Remember to use your best cursive handwriting.

hum, honk, hush

chatter, cluck, knock

creaky, crunchy, jingle

Write on your own paper.

Circle a word you spaced correctly.

Circle a word in which all the letters slant correctly.

103

p p   *p*   *p*   *p*   *p*

Write on your own paper.

p — — — — — *p* — — — — — *p*

p — — — — — *p* — — — — — *p*

picture picture

special step

proud person

104   **SELF CHECK**   Circle a word in which all the letters slant correctly.

b b

b

b Write on your own paper. *b* *b*

b *b* *b*

bi b i bi *big*

a big job

broad boulder

ON YOUR OWN

Describe to a partner what you think the moon looks like.
Have your partner draw a picture to fit your description.

_w_ _w_ _w_

1 _w_ 2 _w_ 3 _w_ 4 _w_

_w_

Write on your own paper.

_w_ _____ _____ _____ _w_ _____ _____ _____ _w_

_w_ _____ _____ _____ _w_ _____ _____ _____ _w_

_wh_ _w_ _h_ _wh_ _where_

who knows where

whose shadow

ON YOUR OWN
Dip a paintbrush tip into water. Use the paintbrush to
practice writing _w_'s on a chalkboard.

Writing Connection: Book Report
Theme: Moon Landing

f f

f f f

f

f Write on your own paper. f f

f f f

flag flag fine feeling

faraway flag

ASK A FRIEND Have a friend circle your best f.

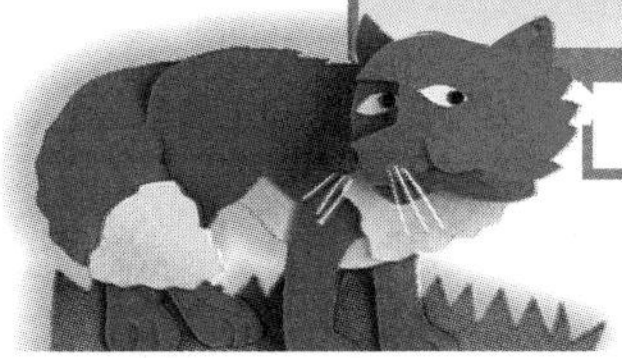

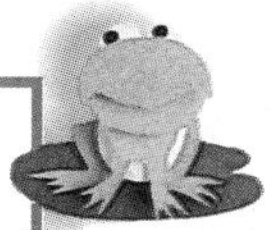

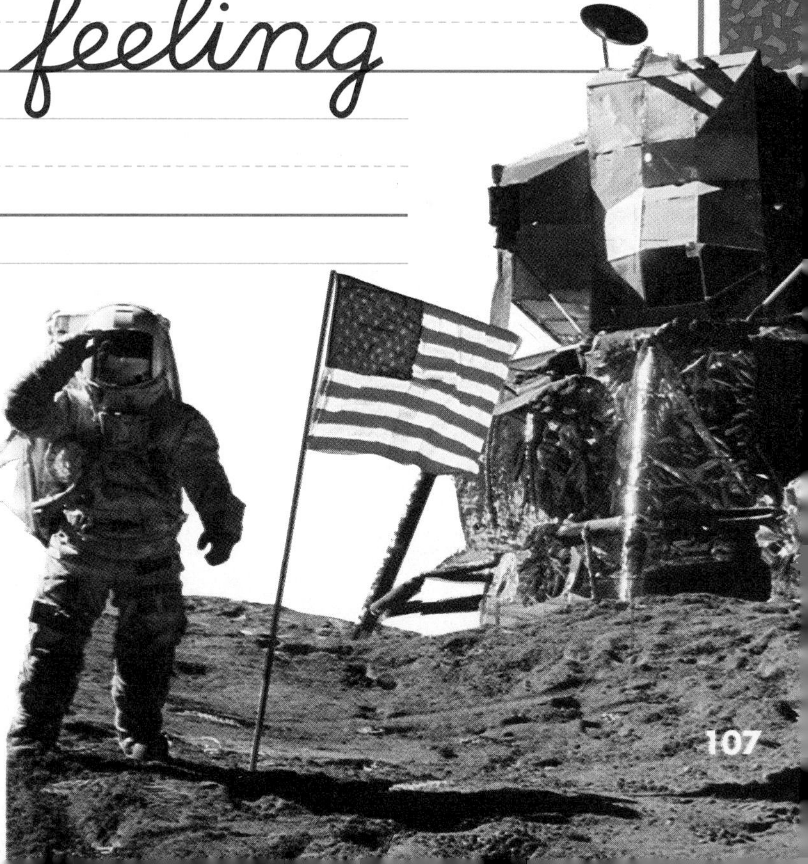

Linking Handwriting to Writing

Writing a Book Report

To Space and Back
by Sally Ride and Susan Okie

The book I read is about

astronauts in outer space.

From this book, I learned

you can float from one place to another.

This book made me want to

go to the moon.

108

Copy the book report.

This book is about

From this book, I learned

This book made me want to

To Space and Back
by Sally Ride and Susan Okie

Write on your own paper.

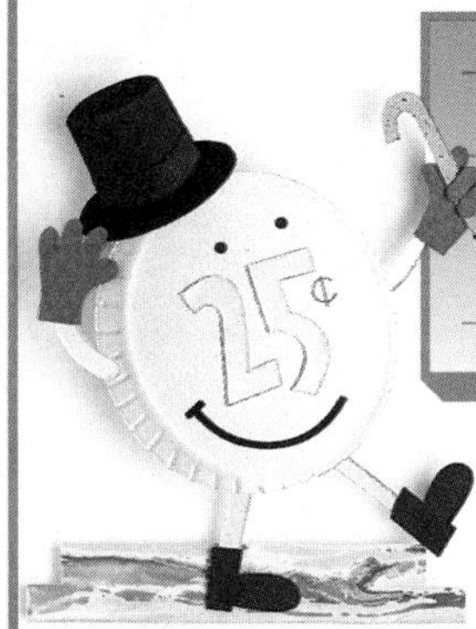

q q

q q q

q

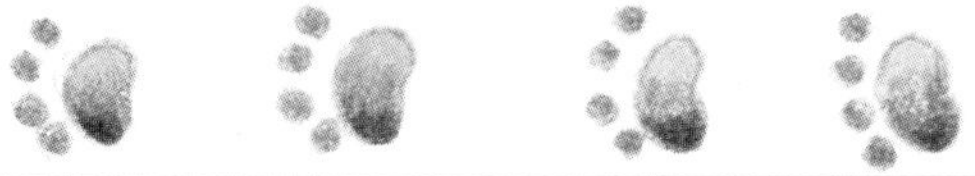

Write on your own paper.

q   q   q

q   q   q

quart quart

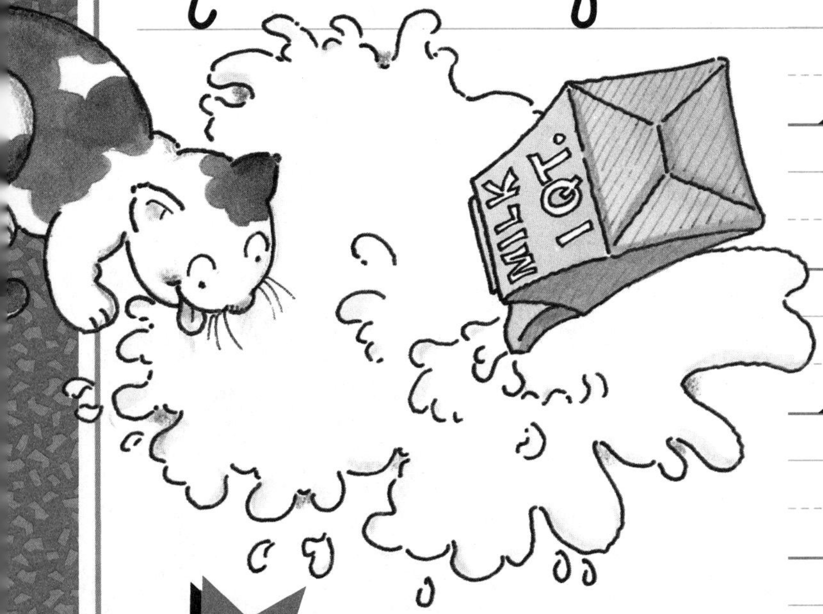

a quart of liquid

some questions

MILK 1QT.

110   **SELF CHECK**   Circle a word that is spaced correctly.

x

Write on your own paper.

x _____ x _____ x

x _____ x _____ x

mix mix

exploring matter

next experiment

ON YOUR OWN   Half fill a clear glass with water. Blow into the water with a straw. Write about what happens.

v $\mathcal{v}$

Write on your own paper.

$\mathcal{v}$ _ _ _ _ $\mathcal{v}$ _ _ _ _ $\mathcal{v}$

$\mathcal{v}$ _ _ _ _ $\mathcal{v}$ _ _ _ _ $\mathcal{v}$

visible visible

invisible gas

moving air

ON YOUR OWN   Try to blow a crayon and a feather from your desktop. Tell which object is easier to move.

Z z

z

Write on your own paper.

z — — — — *z* — — — — *z*

z — — — — *z* — — — — *z*

zero zero

frozen solid

a great size

ASK A FRIEND Have a friend circle your best word.

113

Linking Handwriting to Writing

Writing Science Notes

Copy the information in the notes below.

solids take up space	liquids flow	gases usually unseen

solids	liquids	gases
Write on your own paper.		

ON YOUR OWN Use your index finger to write words on a tray covered with sand.

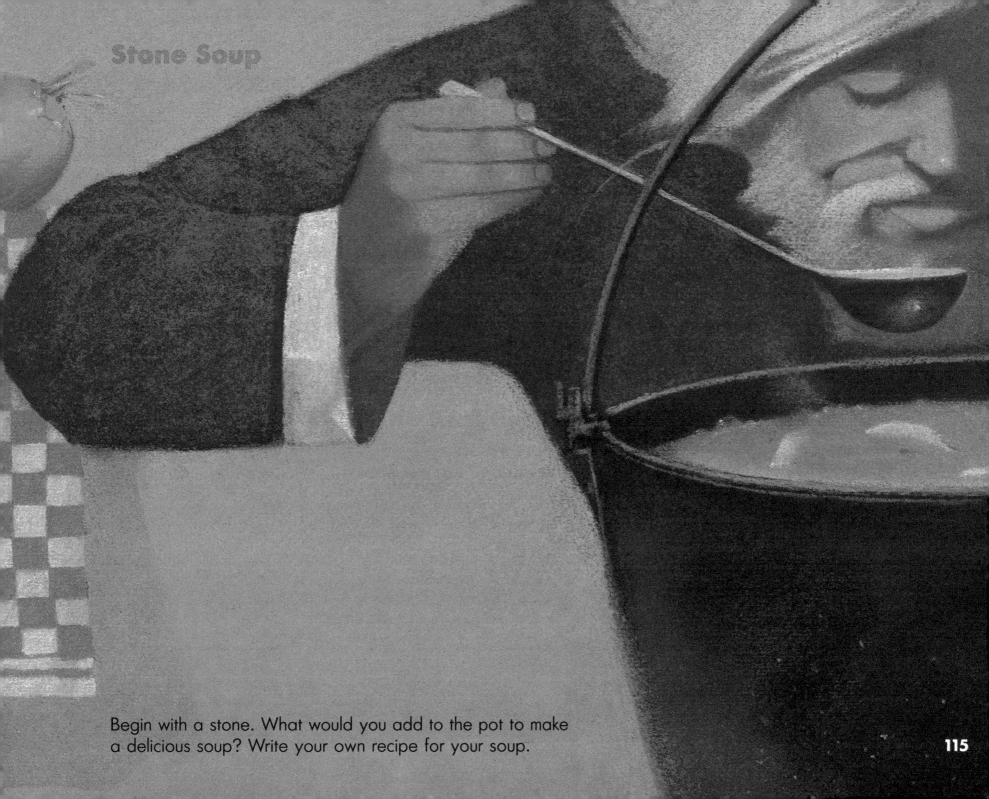

Begin with a stone. What would you add to the pot to make
a delicious soup? Write your own recipe for your soup.

115

Copy these phrases. Remember to use your best cursive handwriting.

fizzing liquid

answers to big questions

everything explained

Write on your own paper.

Circle a word you spaced correctly.

Circle a word in which all the letters are spaced correctly.

Writing to Celebrate

It's a Party!

Date: July 14

Time: 12 noon

Place: Meet at Mark's
We're going to a
ball game!

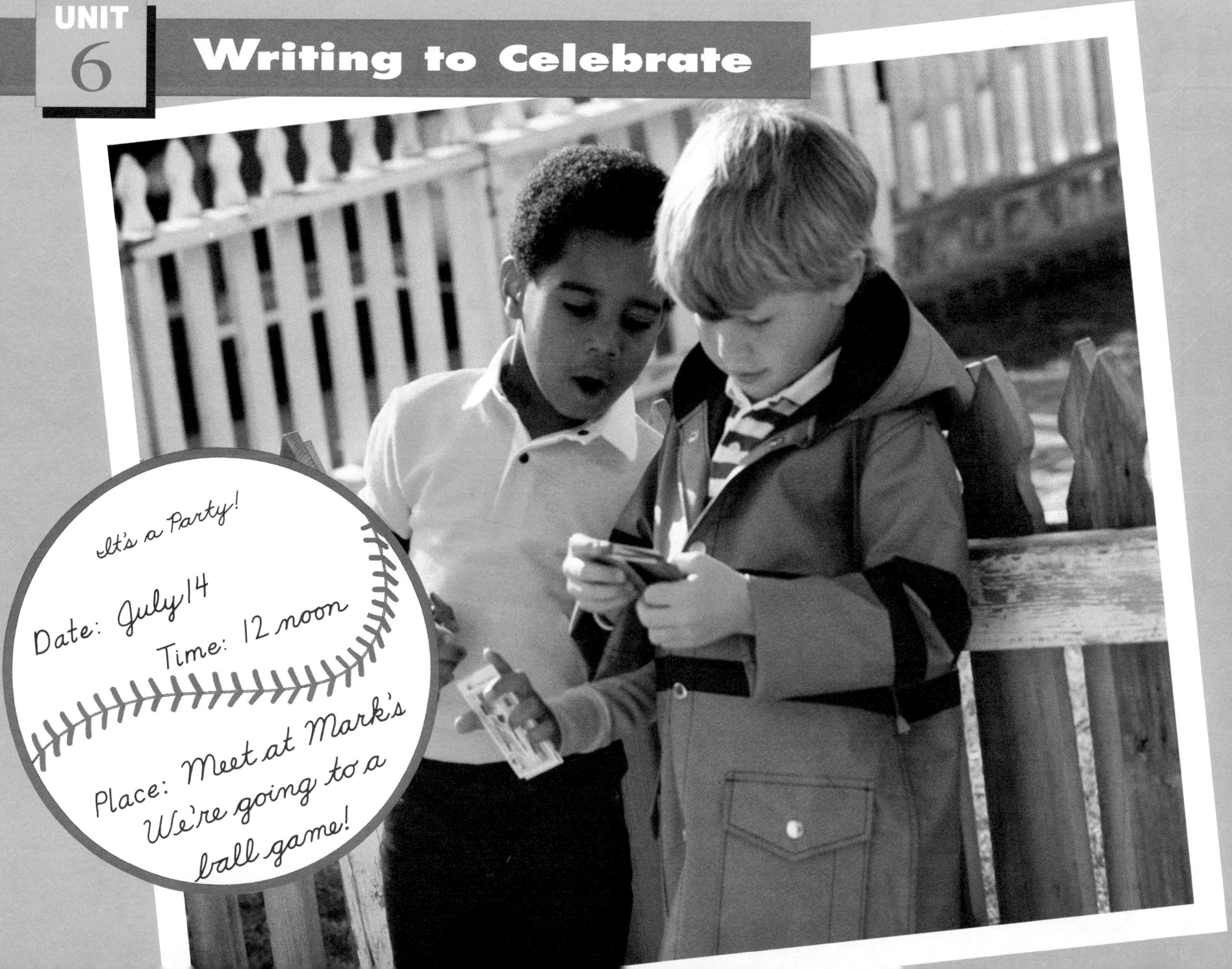

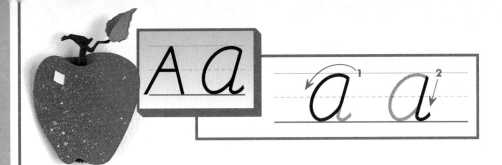

A a

a a a

a

a ⎯⎯⎯ a ⎯⎯⎯ a

Write on your own paper.

a ⎯⎯⎯ a ⎯⎯⎯ a

April 10 is the birthday
of Andy Adam Ames.

 ON YOUR OWN

Find out the next birthday in your family. Circle the date
on a calendar to help you remember that special date.

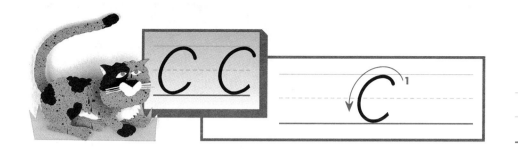

C C

C^1

C

C   Write on your own paper.   C   C

C   C   C

Carla mailed invitations.

Come and celebrate!

 SELF CHECK   Circle your best C.

119

$\mathcal{E}$ $\mathcal{E}^1$ $\mathcal{E}^2$

$\mathcal{E}$

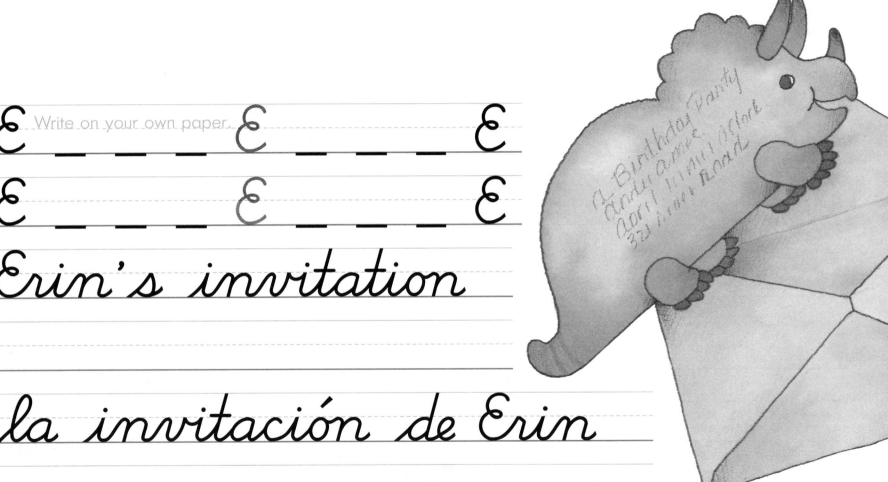

$\mathcal{E}$ Write on your own paper. $\mathcal{E}$ $\mathcal{E}$

$\mathcal{E}$ _ _ _ _ _ $\mathcal{E}$ _ _ _ _ _ $\mathcal{E}$

Erin's invitation

la invitación de Erin

ASK A FRIEND Have a friend circle any $\mathcal{E}$'s that need improvement because they do not loop at the midline.

OO

O

Write on your own paper.

O   O   O

O   O   O

Owen will go too.

Owen asistirá también.

Andy's Party

9   10   17

Q Q

Q

Q Write on your own paper. Q Q

Q Q Q

Quinn and Quiana chose a birthday gift.

122 **SELF CHECK** Circle your best Q.

𝓑 Write on your own paper. 𝓑 𝓑

𝓑 𝓑 𝓑

Ben is wrapping the gift.

Be careful, Ben.

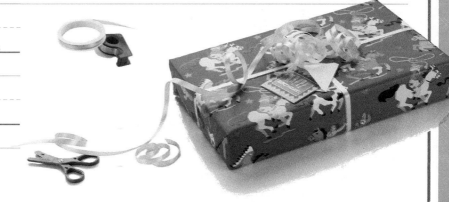

ON YOUR OWN

Make your own special wrapping paper. Decorate the paper with the initials of the person who will receive the gift.

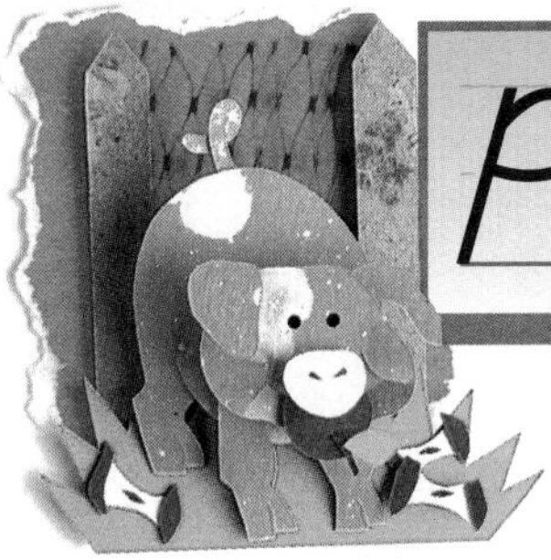

P p

Writing Connection: Invitation
Theme: Birthday Party

P

P Write on your own paper. P P
P P P

Perry will bring
a Punchy Pal.

ASK A FRIEND Have a friend circle your best P.

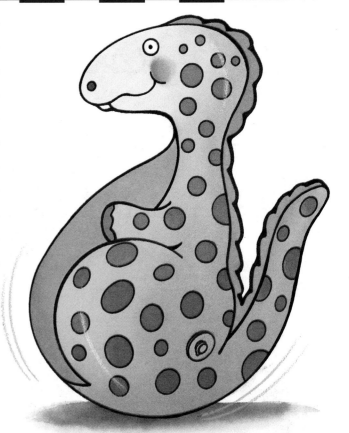

R R R R R

R Write on your own paper. *R* *R*

R *R* *R*

*Roxy will bring her
Rita Reptile video.*

ON YOUR OWN

Write two sentences about your favorite video. Tell the title of the video and why you like watching it.

125

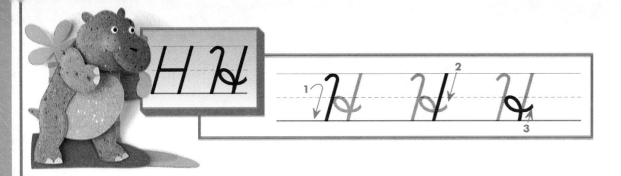

H H

H   Write on your own paper.   H   H

H   H   H

Here is a card.

Happy Birthday!

Have fun!

★ **ON YOUR OWN**   Make a birthday card with a special message for a friend or family member.

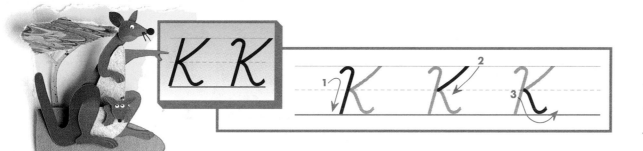

K K K

K

K   K   K

K   K   K

Keep playing games.

Andy's party is OK!

SELF CHECK   Circle a word you wrote smoothly.

127

Using Punctuation

The Comma

Use a comma in dates. It separates the day from the year.

Write on your own paper.

April 5, 1995

Use a comma in addresses. It separates the city from the state.

Oahu, Hawaii

Sometimes you list three or more things in a sentence. Use a comma to separate the things.

Here are my toys, games, and books.

128 ON YOUR OWN Look in a book to find a place where commas are used. Copy the sentence.

Using Punctuation

The Exclamation Point

A sentence that shows a strong feeling is an **exclamation.**
Use an exclamation point at the end of an exclamation.

! ------- ! ------- !
Write on your own paper.

A birthday is today!

Balloons are everywhere!

Come on! Open the gifts!

 **ON YOUR OWN** Draw a birthday balloon with a special message on it. Use an exclamation point.

Linking Handwriting to Writing

Writing an Invitation

Proofreading   The box shows proofreading marks you can use to correct mistakes.

Use the marks to change three lowercase letters that should be capitals and one capital that should be lowercase.

Proofreading Marks		
≡	use a capital letter.	k̲aren
/	Change a capital letter to lowercase.	I̸n

Write on your own paper.

A Birthday Party!
Andy ames
April 10 At 1 o'clock
321 river road

🖥 **COMPUTER TIP**   Find the key on the computer keyboard that helps you make capital letters.

Final Draft Copy the invitation from the previous page.
Make the corrections that the proofreading marks show.

HANDWRITING TIP Remember to leave a space as wide
as a pencil between words.

Write on your own paper.

Make a birthday sign! Use liquid glue to write the words *Happy Birthday*.
ON YOUR OWN Then sprinkle confetti or glitter over the words.

131

𝒟

𝒟 Write on your own paper. 𝒟 𝒟 𝒟

𝒟 𝒟 𝒟

𝒟ancers!

𝒟ecorate today.

𝒟ance and sing.

132 **ON YOUR OWN** Look up information about Cinco de Mayo to share with classmates.

𝒯𝒯

𝒯

𝒯   Write on your own paper.   𝒯   𝒯

𝒯   𝒯   𝒯

The music fills the park.

Today is special.

SELF CHECK   Circle your best 𝒯.

133

$\mathcal{F}$

$\mathcal{F}$ Write on your own paper. $\mathcal{F}$ $\mathcal{F}$

$\mathcal{F}$ $\mathcal{F}$ $\mathcal{F}$

Feel the excitement!

Fiesta!

  **ASK A FRIEND**   Ask a friend to circle any $\mathcal{F}$ that isn't crossed.

I $\mathcal{I}$

$\mathcal{I}$

$\mathcal{I}$ Write on your own paper. $\mathcal{I}$ $\mathcal{I}$

$\mathcal{I}$ $\mathcal{I}$ $\mathcal{I}$

Imagine you are there.

It's lively.

ON YOUR OWN Imagine there will be a big party soon in your neighborhood. Make a colorful poster that invites neighbors to the party.

G G

𝒢

𝒢 *Write on your own paper.* 𝒢 𝒢

𝒢 𝒢 𝒢

Groups gather to hear.

Get ready.

136 ⭐ **SELF CHECK** Circle a 𝒢 you wrote smoothly.

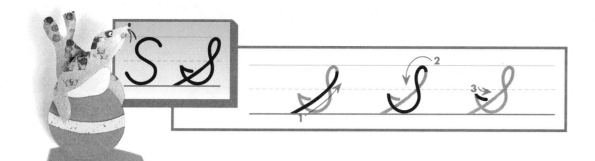

$\mathcal{S}$ $\mathcal{S}$

$\mathcal{S}$

$\mathcal{S}$ Write on your own paper. $\mathcal{S}$ $\mathcal{S}$

$\mathcal{S}$ $\mathcal{S}$ $\mathcal{S}$

Shush!

Stop and listen.

Sweet music plays.

ON YOUR OWN What is your favorite musical instrument? Write a paragraph to describe it.

137

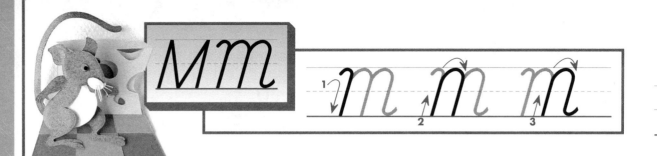

Mm

m m m m

m Write on your own paper. m m

m m m

Cinco de Mayo is here.

May 5

  **ON YOUR OWN**   Circle your best m.

$\mathcal{N}\,n$

n $\hat{n}$ n

n n Write on your own paper. n n

n n n

n n n

Neighbors come together.

New friends share.

ON YOUR OWN

How does your family or neighborhood celebrate a holiday?
Write a paragraph to describe the celebration.

139

Linking Handwriting to Writing

Writing a Thank-You Note

Copy the thank-you note on your paper. Do not copy the words in blue.

Heading

May 8, 1994

Greeting

Dear Teresa,

Body

Thank you for taking me to the fiesta. I really had fun.

Closing

Gracias,

Signature

Sara

140 **ON YOUR OWN** Write a thank-you note to someone who has done something you appreciate.

Copy these sentences. Remember to use your best cursive handwriting.

Hey! I hear music.
A fiesta is starting.
Put on a costume.
Diego will bring Chiang.

Write on your own paper.

Circle the letter you wrote best.

Circle a word you wrote smoothly.

J J

J J J

J

J   Write on your own paper.   J   J

J   J   J

Jin is on the team.

Jeri plays too.

142   SELF CHECK   Circle your best J.

$\mathscr{L}$ $\mathscr{L}$ $\mathscr{L}$

$\mathscr{L}$

$\mathscr{L}$ Write on your own paper. $\mathscr{L}$ $\mathscr{L}$

$\mathscr{L}$ $\mathscr{L}$ $\mathscr{L}$

Left field is Libby's spot.

Let's play!

$\mathcal{U}$ $\mathcal{U}$

$\mathcal{U}$ $\mathcal{U}$

$\mathcal{U}$

$\mathcal{U}$ Write on your own paper. $\mathcal{U}$ $\mathcal{U}$

$\mathcal{U}$ $\mathcal{U}$ $\mathcal{U}$

Umpire Upton signals.

Ursula is safe!

ASK A FRIEND

Have a friend circle any $\mathcal{u}$ that needs improvement because it doesn't end just above the baseline.

V U

U

U

U   U   U

U   U   U

Write on your own paper.

Vince hit a home run.

The Volcanoes win!

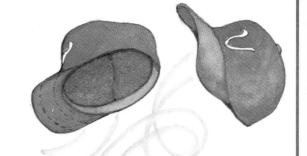

Victory!

ON YOUR OWN   Imagine you are a reporter. Interview a partner who pretends to be a sports star.

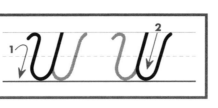

Writing Connection: Friendly Letter
Theme: Softball

$\mathcal{W}$

$\mathcal{W}$ Write on your own paper. $\mathcal{W}$ $\mathcal{W}$

$\mathcal{W}$ $\mathcal{W}$ $\mathcal{W}$

We win! We win!

We're number one!

Wow!

  **SELF CHECK** Circle a $\mathcal{W}$ you wrote smoothly.

Writing Connection: Friendly Letter
Theme: Softball

X X

$\mathcal{X}$ X

$\mathcal{X}$

$\mathcal{X}$ Write on your own paper. $\mathcal{X}$ $\mathcal{X}$

$\mathcal{X}$ $\mathcal{X}$ $\mathcal{X}$

Xavier cheers.

Coach Xin laughs.

⭐ **ON YOUR OWN**   Use long pieces of colorful yarn to form $\mathcal{X}$'s.

Y

Writing Connection: Friendly Letter
Theme: Softball

Write on your own paper.

Y Y Y Y Y Y

Yes, let's celebrate.

You can come, Yuri.

148 ASK A FRIEND Have a friend circle your best Y.

Z z

Write on your own paper.

We beat the Zane Zebras.

Zak took pictures.

 **ON YOUR OWN** Write a cheer for a favorite sports team. Tape-record your cheer with some classmates.

Linking Handwriting to Writing

Writing a Friendly Letter

Read the letter.

Heading July 6, 1994

Greeting
Dear Grandpa,

Body
Boy, did you miss a
big game! I hit a
home run for you.

Closing
Love,

Signature
Vince

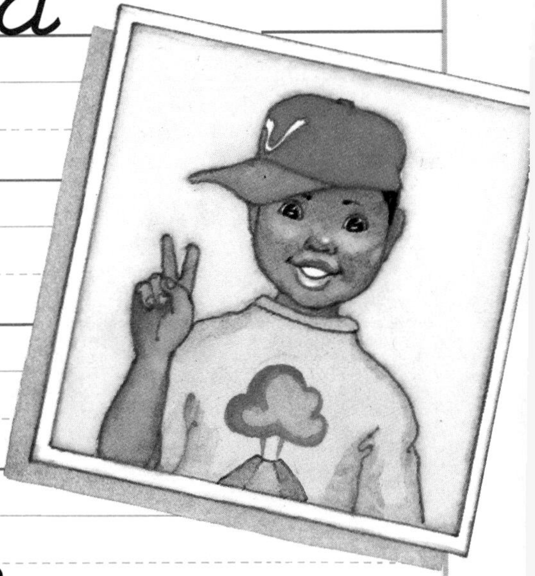

Copy the letter that is on page 150. Do not copy the words in blue.

Write on your own paper.

ON YOUR OWN Think of someone who missed one of your very happy times. Share that time
by sending a friendly letter and a photograph or drawing to that person.

The address on an envelope shows where the letter goes. Every address has the following.

1. The name of the person getting the letter
2. The number of the house and the name of the street
3. The city, the state, and the ZIP code

Copy the address on your paper.

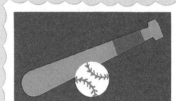

Mr. Len Jackson
807 Vernon Lane
Toledo, OH 43624

ON YOUR OWN

Write the name and address of someone you would like to send a letter to, or write your own name and address.

You probably have a special way of tossing a ball. First, you learned the correct way to toss a ball. Next, you practiced it until you could do it easily. Then, you discovered you could toss a ball in a way that was both correct and all your own. You could do it by using your **personal style**.

You can use your personal style in handwriting too. Look closely at the words below. Notice the sizes of the letters in the first row and the slant of the letters in the next row.

wide   narrow

right   left   straight

Use your personal style to write the word *ringmaster*.

Write on your own paper.

Copy these sentences. Remember to use your best cursive handwriting.

Join the Volcanoes.
Whip the Zebras.
Lin is out! Unfair!
Yea! Xenon has a hit!

Write on your own paper.

Circle the capital letter you wrote best.

Circle a word you wrote smoothly.

On your own paper, copy the poem "Writing on the Chalkboard" by Isabel Joshlin Glaser. Begin with the title. Use your best **cursive** handwriting.

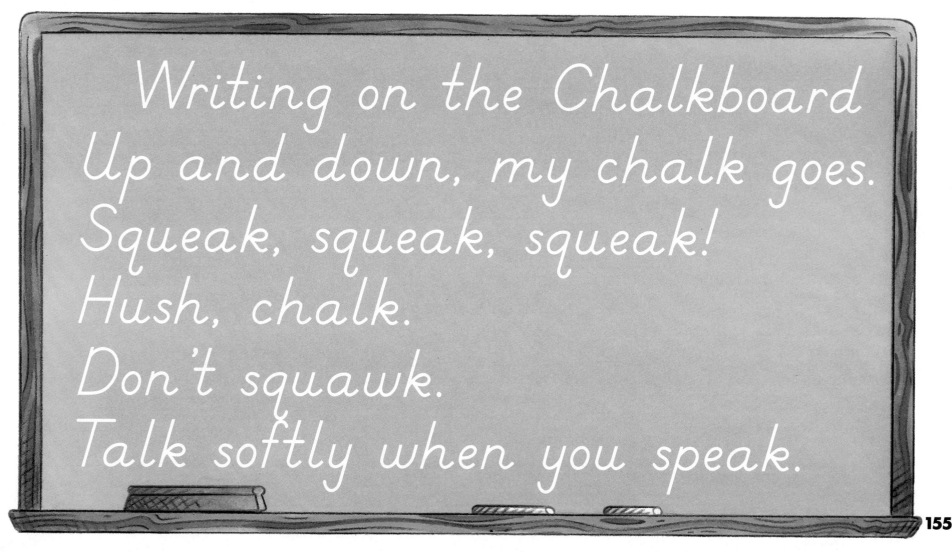

Writing on the Chalkboard
Up and down, my chalk goes.
Squeak, squeak, squeak!
Hush, chalk.
Don't squawk.
Talk softly when you speak.

Index